# COUNTRY HOUSES
## AND HOW TO BUILD THEM

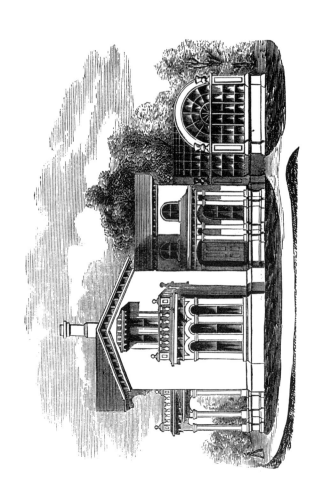

# COUNTRY HOUSES

### AND HOW TO BUILD THEM

---

DANIEL T. ATWOOD

---

THE LYONS PRESS

Originally published in 1871 by Orange Judd & Co.

First Lyons Press edition, April 2001

Printed in the United States of America

2  4  6  8  10  9  7  5  3  1

Library of Congress Cataloging-in-Publication Data is available on file.

TO

# THE SEEKING MILLIONS

## 𝔚𝔥𝔬𝔰𝔢 𝔍𝔞𝔦𝔱𝔥 𝔦𝔫, 𝔞𝔫𝔡 𝔏𝔬𝔳𝔢 𝔣𝔬𝔯 𝔞 𝔥𝔬𝔪𝔢

LIGHTENS

## EVERY TOIL AND SELF-DENIAL

EXERTED IN ITS BEHALF,

THIS WORK IS INSCRIBED

BY THE

AUTHOR.

# PREFACE.

SOME apology seems due to the friends of the author who have been delayed in the receipt of Country Houses much beyond the time appointed. Also for the publication of a less number of designs than was first promised.

A desire not to increase the size of the present book beyond a certain number of pages, induced the Author to reserve a number of designs of Villas and Cottages, built in various parts of the country, for a second series now in preparation, with such improvements, in plates, details, and specifications, as will give greater suggestive and practical value.

The interest and love manifested by all classes for tasteful homes in the country, may be regarded as one of the happy results of our united American civilization, and it is a cause of sincere thanksgiving that a policy of government, so wise and liberal in its principles, has been maintained, in whose bounteous soil the sentiment for home beauty has been propagated, and become so universal among all classes of our fellow countrymen.

It is to contribute something toward the practical shaping of this interest that the Author supplies the public with these hints and suggestions as to the general principles of house building, style, cost, location, symmetry and modes of building, and believes his humble labors will not be in vain.

DANIEL T. ATWOOD.

# CONTENTS.

## CONTENTS. 11

# COUNTRY HOUSES.

## HINTS TO HOUSE SEEKERS—CHOOSING THE SITE.

———◦◦⦂◦⦂◦◦———

HE site for a dwelling should combine, as far as possible, health, convenience of access, agreeable views, and shelter, or some natural protection from northerly winds. I should consider a site desirable if supplied with an abundance of good water, naturally or by the sinking of wells, if situated in a gently undulating or rolling country, whose soil is light and fertile, adapted to a generous culture, and the atmosphere generally pure and salubrious, the roadways direct and ample, and the northerly exposure protected rather by trees than hills, which afford cool and refreshing breezes in summer.

Most persons know the advantages arising from the possession of a good site for the dwelling; the ease with which it may be disposed of in time of need, together with the enjoyment which its possession confers. It is quite as well known that if the best natural qualities of a site are wanting, nothing that can be done by artificial means will quite supply their place ; you may rear a costly and elegant house, lay out walks, do planting, and employ the most ingenious artifices of the landscape engineer's art, and not then cover the deficiencies of a poor site.

You may on the other hand select a naturally good site, build commonplace buildings, indulge in little expense, pay but little attention to the rules of art, and have a home incomparably better and more attractive; simply because it is associated with natural advantages, and avails itself of natural beauty.

Use caution, therefore, instead of haste in making your selection; examine not only two or three, but all the places within the range of your ability to possess; ask questions freely, and seek advice from persons of experience and judgment. Concerning any particular locality, propound these queries: Do the statistics of the longevity of the inhabitants of this quarter show the average run of life? Is the air wholesome and pure, the soil gravelly or loamy and moderately high and rolling? Is the water limpid and abundant? Vegetation, full and healthy? Is the locality free from miasmatic influence? [And it would be well to inquire also if it is free from mosquitoes.] If affirmative answers be given in whole, or even in part, you may class it as eligible.

### THE PLAN.

Next in importance to the choice of a *site* is the selection of a *plan;* its extent being governed by the amount to be expended, the chief point in its management should be studied with particular reference to convenience and the exposures at hand.

Sleeping rooms should be provided with an easterly exposure on account of the morning light and a cooler temperature at night, which in midsummer is very desirable.

A northeasterly or southwesterly exposure is best for parlors or sitting rooms, a northerly for the kitchen and its offices, or closets and store rooms, a southerly for study, or library, and dressing rooms.

No plan is complete or a good one that does not, in proportion to its limits, provide ample closet space for the sleeping rooms, pantries for the kitchen and dining room, with stairs and passages for communication with all the principal rooms, centrally located. The ordinary passages should be not less than $3\frac{1}{2}$ feet, and properly lighted and ventilated. Entrance halls with an open staircase in cottage houses should be not less then $6\frac{1}{2}$ feet wide. The kitchen conveniences should be made perfect in their kind.—The kitchen is the engine room of the whole household.—It is here you will bake, brew, and wash, and perform a daily round of labor essential to the order, cleanliness and comfort of the whole family. It is therefore necessary to provide, as of first importance,

## A WATER SUPPLY,

from cisterns, or springs, or wells, by means of an apparatus either economic or expensive in its construction according to the means and social habits of the owners. The method most common and inexpensive, is to employ lead pipe and a lift pump, set over an iron or wooden sink, about 20x40 inches, and 6 in. deep, communicating with the cistern or well, with waste pipe passing to an outside drain or cesspool, and properly trapped, as shown in Fig. 1.

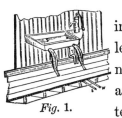

*Fig. 1.*

The sink, which here is of iron and supported on iron legs, may be enclosed underneath with narrow tongued and grooved boards, and painted. T, is the stench-tap, communicating with the waste pipe w, which should discharge by a drain outside into a cesspool. s, is the supply pipe connected with the pump, and communicating with the cistern or well.

2*

Wash Trays are another convenience the kitchen of the middle class cottage is seldom provided with, but should be placed here, whether a full plumbing supply is intended or not; they may be used in connection with the common cistern sink, and supplied by the same pump by being built adjoining it. These should be in two or three divisions of about 20x30 in. each, and provided with a waste pipe to connect with the waste of the sink. The bottom of one of the tubs next to the sink, should be $1\frac{7}{8}$ inches lower than the other, to allow the waste water from the adjoining one to pass into it near the bottom, by removing a plug, and to pass off through the waste pipe, which should communicate with this division only.

Fig. 2. represents a set of trays or tubs which cost no more than the common portable

*Fig. 2.*

tubs, and are always in place and convenient, and being covered can, if kitchen accommodation is limited, be used as a side table. The sides and ends of the trays are made of 2 inch seasoned pine plank, and put together with white lead and nails. The covers should be made of $1\frac{1}{4}$ in. pine, and made to project with a nosing equal to their thickness.

A range breast should be built in the kitchen in all cases, instead of the common stove chimney, since this apartment—usually the most imperfectly ventilated—needs as much attention in this respect as sleeping rooms, in order that the gases and vapor made while the cooking operations are in progress be taken immediately from the room, without exposure to draughts of cold air.

Fig. 3 shows a convenient form of kitchen range breast, 4 feet wide on the first floor of the dwelling, with a flue 8x16 inches.

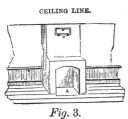

CEILING LINE.

*Fig. 3.*

The opening at floor, (A) is designed to accommodate the stove or portable range, which sets under the flue, controlled by a sheet-iron valve, and is raised when it is necessary to convey the fumes of cooking immediately away.

The valve (v), near the ceiling, should be 12 x 16 inches, and self-acting, and is intended for the outward passage of vapor in parts of the room remote from the fire. When it is desired to use any of the stationary ranges in the kitchen, this form of breast must be enlarged in width to conform to the size you wish.

An outside entrance, opening into a wood shed or porch on one side of the fire, and ample light on opposite sides of the room are most desirable. Store pantries should in all cases communicate with the kitchen, and the inner passage to the provision cellar. The dish and china closets should be convenient to both dining room and kitchen, and the communication between these last named apartments should be by a short passage in all possible cases.

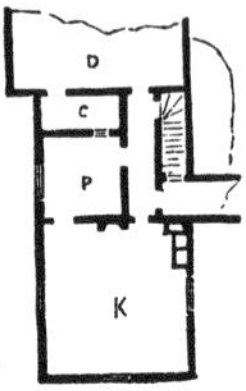

Fig. 4 is a section of a House plan, showing a good arrangement for the middle class house. Chimneys should be located centrally for the

*Fig.* 4.

purpose of retaining all the waste surface heat inside the building, and maintain a better architectural appearance externally.

Doors should be arranged to hang and swing as right-hand doors, and always to lift off, or with loose jointed butts. Their length or height should in all cases be (9-12) nine-twelfths the height of the rooms or height of ceilings, and from 2 ft. 6 in. to 3 ft. wide for single doors, and when double doors are used for the front entrance to a cottage, the folds singly should be 2 ft. 2 in., to 2 ft. 6 in. for any medium sized house; their height 10-12ths of the height of the room, and this width would be proper for entrances into halls and lobbies from 7 to 10 ft. wide. Avoid having too many doors open into one apartment. The number should not exceed three where there are no unusual obstacles in the way of forming the plan and communications from room to room.

When door openings occur on both sides of a pier or mantel breast, the spaces should be equal, in order to preserve the symmetry of that side of the room, as shown in Fig. 5.

*Fig.* 5.

In lighting a dwelling it is an injudicious practice to place more than two windows or openings in one side of a room, and where there are two sides facing any exposure the better practice, both for effect and utility, is to place single lights or openings on a side, either single, double or triple mullioned windows, or some form of bay on one of the sides with a window on the other, allowing for the height of the openings (8-12) eight-twelfths of the height of the ceiling or room, and locating the sill or bottom (2-12) two-twelfths above the floor. If these openings are to remain single, their width should be (2-5) two-fifths the length. This proportion for two windows will give ample light for any ordinary room, and for all rooms, whether oblong or square, containing a superficial area of 384 feet, and about 3840 cubic feet, or for a room about 16 x 24 feet. It is oftentimes desirable for pyramidal effect, and the superimposition of the exterior design to form the window opening into doublets and triplets. In such cases observe the rule above for length, and take (½) one-half the length for the width, the aggregate width being separated into two equal parts by a proper mullion. If for a triplet window, observing the same rule for the length, take (3-5) three-fifths of the same for the width, separating the aggregate light into three equal parts by proper mullions.

Bay and oriel windows are pretty and effective features in any design, and by being located on a southerly exposure may be adapted to floriculture, or growing of house and specimen plants, by the family. This class of window may be employed in the form of a square, a hexagonal, octagonal, or circular projection, and may have two, three, or five lights or apertures. For square bays, the rules given above will apply; their projection from the building being governed according to circumstances, or the will of the designer. For hexagonal, octagonal and round projections, or bays, the width inside should be equivalent to (⅓) one-third the length of that side of the room of which it is to form a part, and the projection from the building should be equal to (½) one-half their respective diameters, the length of openings for lights to be governed by the rule above, and the angles separating the lights, and forming mullions and boxes for weights. The ceilings of all cottage bays should conform to the height of the ceiling in the rooms.

Proportions of rooms should be considered in connection with their use, and the rules regulating the proportions of the exterior and skeleton or frame of the building; and whether designed for comfort and convenience, or to please by their elegance and beauty, some regard to natural harmony should be observed, without which they may offend the most unpracticed eye. The external measurements of a building, including width, length and height, may be adjusted by some of the ratios denominated harmonic and arithmetic proportions of buildings, according to the following rules: For the proportion of the outside of the main portion of the dwelling or any of its additions, first determine the height, or number of stories, by deciding whether you require a (1½) one-and-a-half or a (2) two story house. Choose for the height of a single story never less than 9 feet for any dwelling, and for a medium class not more than 10 or 12 feet; add together the heights of whatever stories selected, including the thickness of floors, and this aggregate height we will assume to be 18 feet. Now, taking the ratio, 6 for the length, 4 for the width, and 3 for the height, we have—

$$3 : 4 :: 18 : 24, \text{ the width,}$$
$$3 : 6 :: 18 : 36, \text{ the length;}$$

or a simpler method may be used by obtaining the greatest common division of 18 feet, which is 6, then the length designated by $6 \times 6 = 36$ feet, the length, and the width $4 \times 6 = 24$ feet, the width.

If the outside of a dwelling is proportioned in the above manner, the principal rooms must partake of the same relative proportions; and in order to fix them more completely, the ratios (3) for the length, (2) for the width, and (1) for the height—and the height of one story, which we assume to be 9 feet, being represented by (1), then—

2

1 : 2 :: 9 : 18 feet, width of room, and

1 : 3 :: 9 : 27 feet, length of room.

There are other ratios besides the above that may be used, accommodating themselves to any measure thought most convenient, consisting of seven numbers in all, which have been termed by an ingenious and able architectural writer as the seven varieties of architectural proportion. It is not expected that any but experienced architects would thoroughly apply these harmonic rules in forming the plan and external design, yet the novice cannot help working out some good results.

The bath room, either for hot or cold water, should be included in the plan of every dwelling, however humble, and if the expense of modern bathing apparatus cannot be indulged, then supply your room with a portable tub, coarse towels and a sponge, which will answer quite as well—consulting your physician or some reliable medical work on the methods enjoined for the hand-bath.

In concluding the remarks on the plan, I may say, no plan will be complete or commendable that does not provide ample means for ventilating the rooms—a subject which will be briefly treated of in another chapter.

## THE STYLE.

In good, "or well building," some attention should be given to the style, as no person of any refinement or culture, however limited in means or unambitious with regard to the extent of his dwelling, would remain content inside of four walls so ordered and arranged as to barely fulfill the requirements of utility—a shelter from storm and heat, a lodging and eating place simply.

As social beings, we are required to rebuke and banish that selfishness which would lead us to build only for our own convenience, and neglect to render that dutiful courtesy in building, intended to please, excite and compliment the taste. As moral beings, we require that buildings should be expressive, and yield definite emotions, indicating their quality and their purpose. And as intellectual beings, we require the refinement of "courtesy into positive beauty, by attention of whatever may please the mind, and preference for whatever may please its highest faculties before that which may please the lower, when they are incompatible, the justice of this preference constituting the difference between right and wrong in art, commonly called good and bad "*taste*." For this reason we demand forms well proportioned, fitting forms, and forms possessing grace and beauty.

There is no good or needful cause for building our cottage houses out of proportion, as many do, or even out of the precincts of some recognized style in architecture. On the plea of cost there is surely none, for the difference in the expense of a box and a building architecturally treated is too trifling to mention, in comparison with the immense advantage and satisfaction gained. And who does not prefer a good form, generously projecting roof cornices, ample windows and entrances, inviting piazzas, and cosy interior.

It is not necessary to enumerate various styles of building here, but with regard to the style suited to a particular locality the following general principles should govern in the selection:

First, choose the style or general features of it to accord with the site and be in harmony, and in some particular in contrast, with the general character of its surroundings.

Second, a highly picturesque neighborhood involves a picturesque style of building, with horizontal lines in contrast to perpendicular ones. A level country, symmetrical buildings; a ridgy country, irregular buildings; a monotonous country, regular buildings. A picturesque site or locality is distinguished chiefly by angular, perpendicular, and diagonal lines, which express strength, stability, and complete beauty of form. Therefore, the styles denominated Gothic, Anglo-Italian, (the former against a back ground of hills, the latter on natural and elevated terraces) or some modifications of them, with the early English and Swiss cottage styles could be suitably employed. A level country is distinguished by level and variously winding lines, expressing ease, variety, and uniformity, and here may be located that variety of nameless styles, modifications of almost every known style; yet many of them examples of taste and refinement.

All buildings, of whatever class, should be made expressive of character in harmony with their use. Dwellings, for example, should express home traits, cheerfulness, comfort, and repose, by giving the requisite attention to their architectural detail, to views, to the lights or placing of windows and doors, ample projections, verandahs, and bays.

### THE FOUNDATIONS.

Foundations may be constructed of brick, stone, and concrete. When brick is employed, use only hard burned ones, and lay them in cement mortar below the ground, using either English or Flemish bond. For medium class dwellings a brick foundation wall, 8 inches thick, will answer, started upon proper footings of stone. All foundations and cellar walls should be built enough below the surface of the ground to avoid being displaced by the frost; 20 to 24

inches will be a sufficient depth for foundations
in a gravelly or sandy soil; and 30 to 38 inches
in a clay or damp soil. "Rubble stone"
(rough quarry stone) foundation or cellar walls
should be 18 inches thick to supply a firm bond.
Concrete foundation walls should be 18 to 24
inches thick. All foundations or cellar walls
should be built upon footings constructed in
such a manner as to drain them of surface water, should any settle down; and, as an additional precaution, select a situation undulating
and dry as possible, that there may exist less
cause for decay in the building next to the
foundation. When cellars are not built, the
enclosure formed under a building, by the
foundations, should be ventilated, and the
loose upper soil removed. The depth of foundations below the ground is sometimes proportioned to the height or altitude of the building
—one-sixth of the altitude for that of the foundations above the footings. This rule, however, is not at all times to be relied on, because
some soils are wet, and some dry, and require
to be trenched deeper, or more shallow, ac-

cording to circumstances, the actual distance
below the surface being determined by the
action of the frost, in either of the above soils.
These remarks apply particularly to the northern latitudes; any uniform rule like the above
being proper south of 36 degrees of latitude.

*Fig.* 6.

Fig. 6, represents a section of
8 inch brick foundation wall laid
on a footing of round or field
stone.

*Fig.* 7.

Fig. 7, a section of a concrete
wall.

*Fig.* 8.

Fig. 8, a section of rubble
stone wall.    The footings of all
walls should project 4 or 6 inches on either side; if the soil is

dry, the trench can be filled with loose field or
other stone, and the wall then built upon it;
if the soil is wet, then large flat stone, laid in
cement, making a course of 8 or 10 inches in
thickness over the footing course of loose field
stone, would be required.  Bottom excavations
for the trenches should have a fall toward
some corner of the building for water to collect,

and some means of exit provided by drain or cesspool, if the soil is wet enough to require it.

Cisterns should be built below the surface of the ground. A circular form is best, and for ordinary family uses, 8 feet in diameter, and 8 feet deep is a good size, excavating deep enough to finish the arch about 20 inches below grade level. One 4-inch course of brick will form the walls of a cistern below ground —the covering should, in most cases, be of brick, arched over in the form of a segment leaving a ''man hole'' about 24 inches in diameter in the middle, the neck of which should be built up to the surface of the ground, and covered with plank or a flag-stone cover. Such a cistern requires two coats of grout on the bottom, and two coats of water-lime cement on the sides and top. The rain-water as it collects on the roof of the house should flow to the cistern through leaders and vitrified 4-inch tile pipe, the latter under ground; an outlet should be provided to take off waste water, communicating with a cesspool, or sand or gravel strata, three or four rods away from the

2*

dwelling.　Cisterns constructed in this manner
can be used as a well by the family, the water
drawn up inside the house by the pump, and
filtered there or in a filter constructed in the
cistern, with pure and foul water compartments—the latter containing the filtering media, through which the rain-water passes and
becomes purified.　The following is a mode
adopted by the author in a number of cases,
with perfect success:

Separate the cistern by a straight 12 inch
brick wall into two equal parts.　Let the 12
inch wall terminate 12 inches below the spring
of the arch.　Plaster the whole interior so as
to make it water tight, and 12 or 15 inches
from the bottom of the pure water compartment, insert a row of two inch cement or vitrified pipe 6 to 8 inches apart, with the inner
ends covered with galvanized iron or plate tin
strainers.

Level with the top of the pipes, and in the
foul water compartment, lay a floor of heavy
slate, quarter of an inch in thickness perforated
with fine one-eighth inch holes, as closely to-

gether as possible. Support the slate floor on blue-stone or granite bearings, and on this provide and lay a filtering media composed of fine slate, charcoal, and screened gravel, in the following proportions: First layer of fine slate 4 inches thick. Charcoal 1 inch thick. Second layer of fine slate 4 inches thick. Layer of screened gravel 6 inches thick, with a flat stone or slate laid to receive the falling water from the inlet. Both the inlet and outlet should communicate with the foul water compartments. Such cisterns should have double covers at the top, and a trap in the outlet drain or overflow about three yards distant.

### THE SUPERSTRUCTURE WALLS.

The superstructure walls, or walls above the foundations, may be built of stone, brick, concrete, or wood; and these different materials thus employed may be used in a variety of ways, accommodating either an economic or expensive mode of building. The most common and inexpensive stone construction is called "rubble work," in which the stones are

*Fig.* 9.

taken from the quarry and laid up without being squared, or worked in any manner, as shown in Fig. 9.

For country houses, this kind of wall may be used with little regard to surface finish—its natural roughness and rustic appearance contrasting finely with undulating surfaces, especially in the midst of vines and shrubs.

A rubble wall may be improved in appearance by introducing as quoins or belting courses, some cut stones like Fig. 10.

*Fig.* 10.

A better class of stone wall, denominated "coursed work," consists of stones squared and laid in regular courses as in Fig. 11.

*Fig.* 11.

Another method is practiced, called "random coursed work," in which the stones are more or less squared, with the joints vertical and horizontal, but placed in irregular courses, as in Fig. 12.

*Fig.* 12.

"Ashlar work," Fig. 13, is still another common method, in which the stone are accurately squared,

*Fig.* 13.

and rubbed, and dressed to given dimensions in length and height, and laid in equal courses, outside a backing of brick, to which they are well anchored.

Walls may be built with a casing of cut stone on both sides, and the middle filled in with rubble or cobble stone. A style of wall may also be built called "fine and wide joint work," commonly styled rustic work. Fig. 14 and Fig. 15.

FINE.        WIDE.

*Fig.* 14.       *Fig.* 15.

There are many other styles of constructing stone walls, ancient and modern. Some with projecting surface, and edges beveled or rounded, or the courses channeled. Some with squarely cut margins of from 1 to $1\frac{1}{2}$ inches all around each stone, leaving the natural rock face exposed. The following are some of the ancient methods, viz.:

"Reticulated" work.—Stones laid diagonally.

"Isodomum" work.—Stones laid in courses, equal thickness and lengths.

"Pseudisodomum" work.—Stones laid in courses, unequal heights, lengths, and thicknesses.

Greek Emplectum, }
Roman      "       } Face stones regular, and the middle filled in with rubble work. Walls very thick.

Long and short work.

Herringbone work.

Brick walls, though not so favorable for the display of the taste and genius of the designer as stone, are deservedly popular, because of their cheapness and dryness, as compared with stone, and the facility with which they may be adapted to a solid or hollow wall construction; in the latter case enabling the mason to spread his mortar or plaster upon the brick for interior finish, and thus save furrings, laths and nails. The ordinary brick superstructure walls are 8 inches, 12 inches, and 16 inches in thickness, and may be laid solid or hollow, and with the "English, Flemish, or Blind bond."

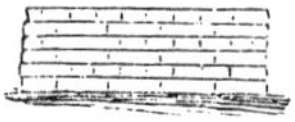

An English bond consists of one course of headers and one course of stretchers alternately. Fig. 16.

*Fig.* 16.

In Flemish bond, every course consists of headers and stretchers alternately, and laid so as to break joints. Fig. 17.

*Fig.* 17.

Blind bond consists of stretchers in every course, with a diagonal header and bond laid every 5th course, but not visible on the face of the wall. Fig. 18.

*Fig.* 18.

The English or Flemish bond makes very strong walls, but is inferior to the Blind bond in appearance. The rule, uniformly observed by modern bricklayers, is to bond every 5th and 7th course, whether the wall be 8 inches, 12 inches, or 16 inches; the headers sometimes appearing on the face of the wall and sometimes concealed from view, according to quality of work.

### BRICK.

When bricks are laid in dry weather, they should be well wet by throwing water upon them, or dipping them before they are used, as this will cause the mortar to adhere, and make firmer work, by giving it time to exert its cohesive properties.

In laying up thin walls, or doing any light brick work where it is important to economize all the strength, this is particularly desirable. During frosty or stormy weather, protect the walls with straw in preference to boards on the top, as expansion takes place after exposure to frost, which render the walls worthless for a number of courses from the top downward.

In laying the walls of a building, they should be carried up together, or nearly so, one side not more than 30 courses in advance of another at any time, on account of their tendency to shrink. This precaution will thus provide for an average shrinkage and avoid dangerous cracks.

### DESCRIPTION OF ANCIENT METHODS.

"The early Greeks constructed their walls—particularly those which surrounded their cities—of rough stones of an immense size; the interstices that were left between these shapeless blocks, were filled with small stones. . . . When the ancients began to cut their stones, they did not cut them rectangular, but gave them an irregular figure of three, four, or six sides, and fitted them together, so that when in their places, they left no interstices between them. The ruins of the ancient wall about the city of Cora, near Velletri, are an example of this mode of building. . . . They next employed stones cut at right angles, and of an oblong form, but their size was not uniform. We find the remains of such walls in Greek and Etruscan buildings. The stones are generally from nine to twenty-two feet long, and from two to six high, in the walls of Volaterra, Cortona, and Pæstum; those of the latter city have been restored by the Romans. Sometimes they gave to the exterior of these stones the form of a rhombus or lozenge, as the ancient walls in the isle of Syria, and in Samos."

As by degrees the Greeks brought their architecture to perfection, they constructed their buildings in a manner more agreeable, more regular, and less gigantic.

There were three different modes of building:—the *isodomum*, which was formed of ranges of large stones of equal height, and which, consequently, gave to the buildings in which it was employed a handsome appearance, and was, therefore, chiefly employed in the construction of temples; the *pseudisodomum*, which consisted of ranges of stones of unequal height; and the *emplectum*, which was employed when it was requisite to give a thickness greater than ordinary to the walls, and in which the outside only of the walls were built up of regular hewn stones, and the interior part filled with rough stones and mortar. For the sake of greater solidity, they placed with care, at certain distances, cross-stones, which served to bind the two outer faces.

The Romans at first imitated the Etruscans

in their manner of building. But in later times, independent of the use of bricks and hewn stones, the Romans had two modes of building, which they called *reticulatum* and *incertum*. The *incertum* consisted in employing the stones just as they came from the quarries, ranged in any order as they could best fit them together. What was called *reticulatum opus*, was a wall composed of square stones, which were not placed in a horizontal direction, but in such a manner, that the junctures lay in a horizontal line, which gave the wall the appearance of net work, whence it received the name of *reticulatum* and was called by the Greeks *dictyotheton*. Vitruvius assures us, that in his time this was the mode of building most commonly practiced. Many edifices of this construction still remain.

The Romans imitated the *emplectum* of the Greeks, but did not execute it with the same care, or solidity.

## CONCRETE WALLS.

In localities where coarse sand and gravel are abundant, the *concrete* or *gravel* wall will be found, in many respects, desirable.    Its chief points of excellence are cheapness, ease of construction, and durability ; and for all buildings of a medium size, in favorable localities, it is preferable to any other.    A prejudice has existed against concrete work, (which fortunately it has nearly "lived down,") on account of a few failures resulting, principally, from want of a proper knowledge of the ingredients and their proper use.

The construction of foundations and superstructure walls, of earth, sand, and gravel, with some cementing medium, as cement or lime, is not new, or very uncommon.    *Pise*, or *en pise*, a species of concrete wall, was practiced at a very early period, in the district of Lyons, France.*    It was also known and

---

* For our climate, it might be found necessary to cover the outside of the walls with a rough cast of cement to protect them.

used to a considerable extent, in Italy and Spain, and, at a more modern date, in England, as illustrated in Woburn Abbey, by the statement of Montbrison. The London *Builder* for 1866 and 1867 contains communications upon the subject of modern concrete building in London and Paris, highly encouraging to us. Four and six-roomed houses for working-men are built there, at a cost extremely low in comparison with our rates for building, and with evident system and thoroughness.

The early Romans employed concrete and *pise* in their vast civil and military works, and nearly every research of antiquity has proven its utility for structural purposes. In some sections of our own country, concrete has been employed for building successfully. I have seen fair models on the line of the Erie Railway, between New York and Goshen. At South Orange, N. J., a large dwelling, octagonal in form, has been built, and, I am informed, is a most successful experiment. Our eminent advocate of social reform, Mr. Fowler, has demonstrat-

ed practically the economy and durability of
concrete walls, by building a dwelling.

In Tompkins County, N. Y., commodious
dwellings have been built, which, in respect to
absorbtion, are superior to any of brick or
stone.

With abundant material for concrete walls,
in every direction from the metropolis, up and
down the Hudson, on the east and west bank,
and for miles back from the Staten Island
shore ; on Long Island, and the slopes of the
Orange mountains ; at Summit, N. J., upon
nearly every building site of Putnam and
Westchester Counties, it seems almost incredible
in view of the great demand for cheap, comfortable and durable houses, that concrete has
not been a favorite material among builders
and house owners.   It is doubtless owing, in
some degree, to the want of skilled labor ; but
skillful laborers for this work will never be
produced by waiting.   The work that is to de-
velop the proper skill should now be begun.*

* In referring to the London *Builder*, for 1866, and later
numbers for 1867, we find the subject of concrete building

ELEMENTS OF A GOOD CONCRETE.

There are three methods of making a good concrete. The ordinary mode, and the one most successful with us, and most economical, where the locality supplies sand and gravel, may be conducted as follows :

If a medium size building, two stories high,

attracting the attention it deserves, for dwelling houses, in both England and France. We quote from a communication to the *Builder*, in June, 1866, by W. E. Newton, a French civil engineer : "Having some important works to carry out in France, I made it my business, some time since, to minutely examine some six-roomed houses, that were being built by Messrs. Tall & Hartley, in concrete, with their patent apparatus. I spent some time at Bexley, in very carefully examining the mode of construction, and in testing their strength, and, although perfectly satisfied, I determined, in order to make assurance doubly sure, to carry on some works under my own eye and superintendence. This I accordingly did, at Norwood, near the Crystal Palace."

As to the strength of concrete walls, he says, "I am now so convinced of the immense strength of concrete walls, and the great economy of the system, that I am about to proceed to carry out my works in Paris on the new plan."

And with reference to the economy, he continues, "I am employing only common day laborers to mix the concrete and fill in the apparatus, and doing all that is required. The plastering, I find, comes to just one-half in labor and materials what is usually paid for brick walls."

then plan to build the wall 12 in. thick; construct moulds of rough 1½ or 2-in. plank, about 8 ft. long, 12 in. wide, and 12 in. deep. If a number of piers are likely to occur, between doors and windows, less than the length of a mould in breadth, then construct some shorter moulds to accomodate these piers as nearly as possible, secure the moulds together, and in their proper position, by fastening the four lower corners with ⅜-inch wrought iron rods with screw thread and nuts on the outer ends, to turn up on the outside faces of the plank, until they are adjusted to the thickness of wall. Secure the tops with iron holdfasts of ¼ x 1 inch wrought iron, to fit down over the top edges of the plank, and made somewhat like a shoemaker's measuring rule with one sliding end to adjust to any thickness of wall,

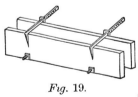

the sliding foot fastened by an iron pin from behind and passing through the horizontal arm, as shown in Fig. 19.

*Fig.* 19.

The mould is disengaged after the wall has

set sufficiently, by turning off the nuts at the bottom on one side, and lifting up the clamps at the top, the rods being drawn out of the wall in removing the other side of the mould.

The concrete may be mixed near the building on the ground, or in the building in a rough mortar box of sufficient capacity to hold an extra mould of concrete in advance of that which is being laid upon the wall.

The ingredients for concrete should be sand, gravel, lime, or cement, in the following proportions:

> Sand, . . . 2 parts.
> Gravel, . . . 6 "
> Lime, . . . 1 "

If cement is used, then proportion in this way:

> Sand, . . . 3 parts.
> Gravel, . . . 6 "
> Cement, . . 1 "

There may be substituted for a portion of the gravel large pebbles, spauls of stone and broken brick. The sand and lime or cement form the cementing substance which binds the

3

mass together, and should be thoroughly worked together with the gravel and stone, as they are thus made to resist greater pressure and wear. Sand should be taken from the pit with only a minimum of loam or earth. The gravel need not generally be screened. Cement is better to mix with than lime, as it produces a concrete of more hydraulic energy, and makes the walls less absorbant of moisture. Limes denominated *poor*, and possessing a proportion of silica and iron, are nearly as good as Roman, Rosendale, or Portland cements.

A much larger proportion of sand and gravel has been employed with the same proportion of lime and cement here designated, giving a wall of medium strength and little hydraulic energy, and requiring a rough-cast outside for protection; 15 to 20 parts sand and gravel to 1 of cement being the proportions used.

Gravel 8 parts, and lime or cement 1 part, have been used, the proportion of gravel being as high in some cases as 12 parts.

Concrete walls may be constructed with a hollow space easily, by inserting a wooden core 1½ or 2 inches thick in the centre of the wall enclosed by each mould, and removing it with the mould, and thus made to possess all the advantages of a hollow brick wall.

Door and window frames should be set and worked up to as the work progresses. The principal corners of the building should be carried up against a scantling, set plumb, and stay-lathed in place, and in working up between these on the sides of the building stretch a line for the outside face, and adjust the mould to it as in stone or brickwork. Scaffolding should be erected on the inside of the walls. The partitions should be carried up with the outside walls, and grounds set for the openings. Bonds should be inserted 1 x 2 inches and 24 inches long, alternated, to receive the interior wooden finish ; at the division of each story, beam plates, 2 x 4 or 5 inches, should be laid to receive the beams, and tie anchors should fasten or tie the trimmers and principal beams and walls together. Wall

plates for the roof should be anchored in the
same manner as in stone or brickwork.  Flues
may be carried up by inserting a round core
with a handle to raise it with the progress of
the wall.  Breasts may be projected into the
room of any width by arching over the fire-
place with brick, and topping out above the
roof with terra-cotta or brick shafts.  If it is
designed to have a cellar, footings of concrete
must be carried 12 inches below the cellar
bottom, and projected 3 inches on each side
of the superstructure walls.  The trenches
should be excavated the exact size and filled
with concrete, and the earth back of the foundations taken off 5 or 6 inches to facilitate the
use of the moulds, and allow room to set and
remove them.  After the walls are completed,
and before they are thoroughly dry, if it is
desired to give the walls a highly finished appearance, the protrusions of concrete at the
junctions of the moulds can be levelled with
the trowel, and a thin coat of rough-cast of
sharp screened sand three parts and cement
one part, plain or colored, can be laid over

the surface and floated evenly down. If the walls are to be left plain, or without the exterior coat, the protrusions on the surface must be removed, and the floating of the surface carried on as the walls are built up.

### AGGLOMERATED CONCRETE.

A second mode of building a concrete wall, consists of first grinding the mass of ingredients together with the addition of less than $\frac{1}{4}$ the quantity of water used for the same bulk in mortar. The grinding is continued until a tough paste is formed, which, placed in the moulds in thin layers and rammed hard, set with rapidity, and become hard as stone. The proportions for this work are as follows :

<blockquote>
Pit sand,     .    .    .   3  parts.<br>
Slaked lime,   .    .    .   1    "<br>
Portland cement,   .   $\frac{1}{4}$    "
</blockquote>

A third mode consists of concrete blocks that may be moulded the thickness of the wall and 24 to 30 inches long, with hollows in the middle of each, or in the form of a common brick, and laid with stretcher and header courses. The ingredients may be the same as for agglomerated concrete, and made in the same proportions. The mass should be mixed or ground together in such a manner that the lime be brought mechanically in contact with the particles of sand, using as little water as possible; and after acquiring the proper consistency it should be placed in moulds and subjected to immense pressure.

A firm in New York city, styled "The American Building Block Company," are manufacturing a concrete block or brick chiefly of lime and sand, of which they speak as follows :

"The Building Blocks are composed of the cheapest known materials—mainly sand and lime—and are made in such form and size, that walls can be constructed from them as cheaply as with good common bricks.

"The shape is entirely uniform, with sharp, well defined lines, and they can be made of every variety of shade, from a pure white to a dark brown or stone color.

"These blocks, as now manufactured, are 10 inches long, 5 inches wide, and 4 inches thick, containing 200 cubic inches, and weighing about 12 pounds each; they have an air chamber running through the centre.

"The blocks, from the nature of the material used, and the severe pressure to which they are subjected in process of manufacture, are very durable in their character, as it is a well known and established fact that mortar composition, properly made, is the most enduring of all substances, withstanding exposure for centuries, and constantly growing harder by atmospheric changes, until it becomes a perfect stone.

"These blocks have been subjected to every conceivable test—have been immersed in water until they have absorbed all the moisture which they could hold, and in that condition they have been exposed to severe frosts, and then thawed, and the same process repeated again and again. After being subjected to all the alternations of the atmosphere, the result in all cases has proved the *indestructibility of the block.*

"They are composed of such materials, that,

so long as the laws of chemistry hold good, time will but make them more durable."

The French, in the district of Lyons, have long practiced a very economical mode of building, with earth and semi-gravel mixture, termed *en pise*, or *pisay*, and with such success as to raise walls three, and even four stories high.

The following abridged description of this method is by Mr. Stewart, from the account of M. Francois Cointereaux, who published a work at Paris, describing *en pise* construction, in 1791 : The manner of operation is merely by compressing earth in moulds or cases, that we may arrive at building houses of any size or height. All earths are fit for the purpose, when they have not the stiffness of clay, or the lightness of poor lands ; all earths which are fit for vegetation; brick earth ; and, more particularly, strong earths with a mixture of small gravel. The following are given as in- dications that the earth is fit for this purpose :

(1) when a spade or plough brings up large lumps of earth at a time ; (2) when arable land lies in clods or lumps ; (3) when field-mice have made their abode in it ; (4) when the roads of a village, having been worn away by the water running continually over and through them, are lower than the contiguous lands, and the sides of these roads support themselves almost upright ; (5) when we find a difficulty in breaking the little clods of earth in the road with the finger ; and (6) whenever deep ruts are observed in the road. In digging cellars and trenches for building, it most commonly happens that what comes out of them is fit for this purpose. When the earth that is near at hand is not of the proper kind, it may often be rendered so by mixing. The principle of mixing is very simple ; strong earths must be mixed with light, those in which clay predominates with others that are composed more of sand, those of a rich gluti-nous substance with others poorer and more barren. The proportion of the mixture must be determined by the degree in which these

3*

different qualities prevail, and must be learned
by practice. With the earth may be mixed
some small pebbles, gravel, rubbish of mortar,
etc.; but all animal or vegetable substances,
or anything liable to corruption, must be carefully excluded. Well worked earth, in which
there is a mixture of gravel, in about two
years' time becomes so hard, that a chisel must
be applied to break it, as though it were freestone.

The following is one of the experiments re-
commended to ascertain the goodness of the
earth: Take a wooden tub without a bottom,
dig a hole in the ground, fix a flat piece of
stone level at the bottom, place the tub on it
and ram it tight all round with earth; then
ram into the tub the earth you intend to try
(which must be dug from a little below the
surface of the ground, that it may not be too
dry or too moist,) putting in at each time
about the thickness of three or four finger
breadths, ramming it well in, till it is filled up
to the brim; make the earth at the surface of
the tub perfectly smooth and even; then take

up the tub from out of the ground, with the earth, or *pise*, in it ; turn the tub upside down, and let the *pise* out, or, if it should stick fast, let it dry in the air for twenty-four hours, when you will find it loose enough to drop out of itself ; keep this lump of pise exposed to the air, but sheltered from any rain that might chance to fall, and if it continue without cracking or crumbling, and increase daily in density and compactness, it is a certain proof that it is fit for building. If the earth be not well pressed round the outside of the tub while filling, the pressure of that which you are ramming in the inside will assuredly burst it, even though the hoops be of iron. The earth, as dug up for *pise*, should be well raked with a rake of about an inch and a half between each tooth, so as to leave in it the small stones and pebbles, which are no larger than a walnut, as they will add to the strength of the mass. In mixing different kinds of earth, a portion of each should be thrown alternately on the heap, in the proportions found requisite, whilst another person mixes them together. No more

earth should be prepared at once than is sufficient for one day's work ; and, if rain be expected, you must have at hand planks or mats
to cover with the moment it begins ; for the
earth can not be used when either too dry or
too wet ; if the latter, the workmen will be
obliged to wait till it has gained its proper
consistency ; if the former, it may easily be
moistened by sprinkling it with a little water ;
when wet in any considerable degree, the
workmen had better stop the work.

The implements used in building *en pise,*
which are few and of very simple construction,
are shown in Fig. 20.

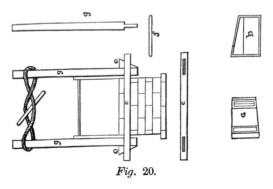

*Fig.* 20.

*a,* is the head of the mould as seen outside ; *b*, the other side as seen inside ; *c*, *c*, the joists in which the upright post is secured by the wedges *e, e ; f*, a round piece of wood called the *wall gauge ; g*, one of the upright posts, with its tenon to enter the mortise in the joist. In our Figure the parts are shown both separately and connected in their places for use.

To make good walls of pise, the earth must not only be well beaten, but they must be well united together. In this mode of construction, in place of the angles or binders of freestone used in buildings, only a few thin pieces of wood is necessary, with a few cramps and nails, to give the greatest solidity. In one single day three courses, each about three feet high, may be raised one over another, forming a wall of about eight or nine feet ; and it has been proved by experience that as soon as the builders have raised their walls to a proper height for the flooring, the heaviest beams and rafters may be placed on the walls when newly made, and that the thickest timber of the roof may be placed on the gables the very instant they are completed. When the first course is laid on the front and inner walls, and before the second course is begun, the evenness and strength of the whole will be increased by placing at the bottom of the mould a board about five or six inches long, and an inch thick, resting on the opposite angle, and so broad that there may remain on each side four or five inches of the earth of the wall, which should be about eighteen inches thick; and the board, being concealed in the body of the pise, will be out of the reach of the air or of damp, and of course there will be no danger of its decaying. The board should be rough from the saw. These boards need only be placed at the angles of exterior walls, and in those parts where the partition walls join it. It is also advisable, particularly where the earth is not of a very good quality, to put ends of planks into the pise, after it has been rammed to about half the height of the mould; they should be only ten or eleven inches long, to leave, as before, a few inches of the earth of the wall on each side. Having determined the height of each story, boards three or four feet long should be placed beforehand in the pise where the beams are to be fixed, and the beams may be laid on for each story, as soon as the mould is moved from the place, the pise being continued as high as the place you intend for the roof. The openings for the doors and windows must be left, as you build the walls, by placing within the mould one or two of the heads of the mould as may be requisite, where the opening is to commence.

They should be made sloping a little, to leave room for the frames and sashes. The chimney pieces are laid in the same manner as common buildings, and the flues are made of brick work, and firmly connected with the walls. The apartments may be very handsomely furnished without making any jambs to the inside doors, as the facings of wood to the earthen wall will render them unnecessary. In making very long walls, as for parks, etc., it will be found requisite to set several moulds to work at the same time in different places, for the sake of speed.

The rich traders of Lyons have no other way than this of building their country houses, and many are known to have lasted for upwards of a hundred and sixty years. An outside covering by painting in fresco, the way most commonly used, entirely conceals the nature of the building, and many of these edifices are extremely handsome. The plaster for the outside of *pise* walls differs from that used on other walls, and it requires to be laid on at a proper time. When a house is begun in February, and completed in April, the covering may be laid on in Autumn, that is, five or six months after it is finished ; if finished in the beginning of November, it may be laid on the ensuing Spring. If it be laid on before the dampness of the wall is gone off, it will be liable to come off. To prepare the walls for plastering, they should be notched with the point of a hatchet or a hammer, the little dents thus made being very near each other. The wall should afterwards be run over with a stiff brush, to detach all loose particles. A scaffold may be quickly erected in the holes which the joists of the mould have left. Two kinds of plaster may be used, rough-cast or stucco. The former consists of a small quantity of mortar diluted with water in a tub, to which a trowel of pure lime is added, so as to make it about the thickness of cream.

Stucco is only poor mortar, made in a clean place near the lime pit, and carried to the masons on the scaffold. The rough-cast is laid on by first sprinkling the wall with a brush, and then dipping another brush made of bits of reed, box, etc., into the rough-cast, which is thrown as equally as possible against the wall; as he lowers the scaffold, the workman can fill up the joist holes with stones, or old plaster, etc.

In stuccoing, one man sprinkles the wall with a brush, and lays on the stucco with a trowel, while another follows him, sprinkles water over the mortar thus laid, and smooths it with a wood flout. It may be whitened with lime as it is laid on.

## WOODEN WALLS.

Wood, so abundant in our country, and so readily adapted to a rapid civilization, is now, and will continue for some time to be, our chief material for domestic buildings of all kinds. Cut into deals and scantlings, it has been accommodated to various modes of construction, some requiring a correct and full knowledge of constructive science, and a skillful execution ; and some easily managed by the simplest rules of carpentry.

Our first experience naturally began with that primitive dwelling so common in the early history of the United States : the "Log House," —a picturesque structure,—the home of the pioneer, and simplest of all wooden wall construction. Examples may now be seen in the newly settled timber regions of the middle and western states, built by the industrious arm and practical good sense of the pioneer woodman and farmer, with a single tool, the ax.

To an advanced type of the log house, as the "hewed face," and inner plastered one, we are indebted for changes and improved modes of construction, from which eventually grew a half dozen other, more modern and perfect styles of wooden wall construction, some of which it is proposed to describe in the following order:

1. The Mortice and Tenon Frame, O. S.
2. The Skeleton Frame, N. S.
3. The Plank Frame.
4. The Skeleton Plank Frame.
5. The Balloon Frame.

Many of the old builders of the present, are familiar with the process of manufacturing a timber frame, old style. The man that could precede his workmen to the forest, armed with square, scratch-awl, and broad-axe, and without a plan delineated upon paper, execute a frame upon the simplest geometrical principles, yet, in accordance with the practice of that day, was held to possess every qualification for a master builder. Naturally enough, the proportions given to the pieces or timbers of the old style frame, were governed by customary and convenient sizes of timber used in the primitive "log house;" and in the "block house," a subsequent and improved style of building with the log, wherever the logs were reduced from a round to a square form by being first "scored," then hewed, and sometimes "counter hewed," and averaging in size 10, 12, and 14 inches.

During an early apprenticeship we have assisted to erect old style timber frames for dwellings and barns, where the chief builders, as a common rule of practice, had no clear idea or intention of adjusting the sizes of the pieces in the frame to the approximate tensile and compressile strains, the building would have to undergo. The precaution was usually taken to obtain without doubt, according to the best judgment in such cases, strength enough, and the well known result was, a huge and massive frame, whose timbers for the principal parts were usually larger than any required for the husk frame of a mill, and hence requiring an unnecessary expenditure of material and labor, and a large force to raise and put it in a perpendicular position.

The sizes of the several parts averaged as follows :

Sills, 10 x 12, 12 x 12, and 12 x 16 inches.

Posts, 8 x 8, 8 x 12, and 10 x 12 inches.

Plates, 6 x 8, 8 x 10, and 12 inches.

Purlins, 6 x 6 and 8 x 10 inches.

Braces, 4 x 4 and 4 x 6 inches.

Studs, 4 x 4 and 4 x 6 inches.

Floor beams, 6 or 8 inches in diameter, with the upper side hewed flat, to receive the flooring. For girths and beams, plate and post sizes were usually employed.

To execute a frame in the old style, requires double the outlay for labor that the modern frame does. End sills are framed into side sills, mortices are "beat" on the top to receive the tenons of the posts, and also for all the vertical posts or studs, 20 to 30 inches, all round. The girths and beams must be mortised likewise on the underside, to receive the upper ends or tenons of the studs, and on the upper sides to receive the studs of the second story. All braces are framed into the posts and the horizontal ties,

beams, or girths, and no studs are allowed to
be cut except above and below braces and
door and window openings. If *hewn timber*
is employed for the frame, all mortices must
be "boxed," and tenons "relished" or "sized,"
an additional item of labor not required for
sawed timber frames.

Except for farm barns, mills for grinding
grain, and for manufacturing purposes, this
mode is nearly obsolete, because it requires a
large amount of labor to execute ; timber,
unnecessarily large, and destroyed some
room, wherever it was necessary to furr off
the walls for the purpose of shutting in the
angles of the posts and beams.

The *Skeleton Frame*, or new style of mortice and tenon frame, built wholly of sawed
timber, is common and popular in all localities, and the mode most frequently and uniformly practiced by builders for every grade
of domestic frame building.

The chief timbers only are mortised and
tenoned, and secured together by seasoned pins
of hard wood. They comprise sills, posts,

girths, ties, and plates, and when raised to proper positions, form the outline, or skeleton of the frame, which is afterwards filled in with story posts or studs, usually (for dwellings) 16 inches from centers all around, cut the exact length, and nailed in three places, top and bottom. Diagonal braces are likewise cut in, and secured with nails. The floor beams of the first story are framed into the sills, 12 and 16 inches from centers. The second and third story floor beams are laid upon the girths, and consequently require no framing. The sizes ordinarily used for this mode, in two and three story dwellings, are as follows:

Sills, 4 x 8 and 6 x 8 inches.

Posts, 4 x 8 inches.

Girths, 4 x 8 inches.

Plates, 4 x 6 and 4 x 8 inches.

Story posts, or filling in studs, 3 x 4 and 2 x 4 inches.

Floor beams, 3 x 9 and 3 x 10 inches.

Studs, doubled about the openings.

These are the ordinary merchantable yard sizes, proportioned to the ordinary requirements of house building, but not wholly suited to special cases in large buildings, either for dwelling or trade purposes, where the strain and weight must be provided for with more care and certainty.   To meet any such special demand in the construction of a frame, the following rules may be employed:

To determine the size of a rectangular post, capable of sustaining a given pressure in the direction of its length.  The constant number or value of pine and of spruce, may be represented by 0,00150, and that of hemlock by 0,00160.

Rule—multiply together the weight or pressure in pounds, the square of the length in feet, and the value, or constant number, for the kind of wood.  Divide this product by the breadth in inches, and the cube root of the quotient will be the thickness in inches.

Example—Let the height of a post of white pine be 10 feet, its breadth 8 inches, and the weight it will be required to carry 5 tons or 10,000 pounds. The constant number or value of pine is 0,00150, therefore, $\frac{10.000 \times 0.00150 \times 10 \times 10}{8}$ $= 188$ nearly, and the cube root of 188 is

5·72 inches: then 5 inches is the thickness required, or a post to bear the above weight should be 5 x 8 inches if 10 feet long.

To find the depth of floor beams of pine or spruce, the length of bearing and breadth or thickness, being given.

Rule—Divide the square of the length in feet by the breadth or thickness in inches, and the cube root of the quotient multiplied by 2·2 will give the depth in inches.

Example—Required the depth of a floor beam of white pine or spruce. The bearing 15 feet and thickness two inches, $\frac{15 \times 15}{2} = 112$ nearly and the cube root of 112 is 4·17 about, *2·2 = 9·174 inches, the depth required for beams 12 inches from centers;*—or 10 inches is near enough for practice ; hence the size of beams required for the above bearing would be 2 x 10 inches in single-joisted floors.

The *Plank Frame* mode is not known in the vicinity of New York City, but builders in the western counties of the State, and portions of

* For miscellaneous rules, see Tredgold's Principles of Carpentry, &c.

4

the West, are familiar with its construction, and esteem it a strong, warm, and economical mode of building.    We have erected several dwellings in this style, and have found them peculiarly adapted for strength and warmth to our naturally severe and changeable climate.    As for facility of construction, the plank frame is not equaled by the celebrated *Balloon Frame* mode.

The following is the manner of building this frame :

Provide and fix sills upon the foundations, as for an ordinary frame; and if the dwelling is to be two stories, or one and a half, use rough, straight-edged hemlock or spruce plank $1\frac{1}{4}$ inches thick; of the required length for the sides, provide and fix over the sills and first floor beams, the second story beams, or girths, of a corresponding size, framed and secured together at the angles, and squared and "staylathed."    Erect at each corner of the frame, two planks plumbed, and securely nailed to the sills, so that the edge of one will "overlap" and nail on the edge of the other.    The edges of both being plumbed before they are finally nailed to the sills. The plank corners, which during the erection of the frame take the place of posts in the ordinary or skeleton frame, are now "stay-lathed" or braced each way with an inch board, and the girths which support the second floor beams, and until now have been lying on the top of the sills, are raised by the aid of "shores," to the height designated for the first story, and there supported until they have been secured at each corner with spikes. Shore up the centers of the girths to keep them crowning, and plank the sides of the frame vertically, edge to edge, all around, nailing into sills and beams. Raise the attic floor in the same manner above the second floor, nailing the loose upper ends to the attic beams, or girths. After which, the projecting ends of plank may be sawed close down to the girths. Rafters may now be placed, and the gable ends planked; after which the openings for windows and outside doors may be laid out on the outer surface, and cut through, large enough to receive the frames respectively. On the interior this frame is furred off with 1-inch battens to lath and plaster upon, as many being placed over the joints of the planking as possible. The outside is trimmed and weather-boarded in the usual manner.

*Skeleton Plank Frame.* This mode differs from the preceding one in the matter of planking only. For this, narrow plank are used $1\frac{1}{2}$ and 2 inches thick, and about 8 inches wide; they are nailed vertically 6 or 8 inches apart all around on the outside of the sills, covered with weather-boards outside, and lathed and plastered inside. For a simple and cheap erection, this mode has met with considerable favor; it is not, however, as warm or as strong as the former mode, but will answer the requirements of construction for cheap one, and one and a half story houses.

The Balloon Frame, thus designated on account of the extreme lightness of some of the scantlings composing the frame, as compared with the mortise and tenon frame, and the absence of all principal timbers, such as sills, girths, beams, and plates, like many other simple modes of building, the balloon style was partly the result of accident and partly of experiment, and was designed as an economical substitute for the old style frame, by nailing pieces together instead of mortising and tenoning them together.

The style is not popular or much used by eastern builders, but has been a favorite system for every class of building in the rapidly growing towns and cities of the West. When and where it became an acknowledged system of wooden wall construction, I am not informed; my first acquaintance with it was in 1855 and 1856, in the neighborhood of Chicago, Ill. At this time a number of Balloon Frames, so called, were being erected in the above place. The mode may be briefly described as follows:

A peculiarity of this frame, is the absence of all tenons and mortises; angles are joined by halving the ends and nailing them together; studs and braces are nailed in their places, and floor beams nailed to bearings and studs for first floors, and to the same studs over bearings, or 1 inch ties, for second and third floors.

After the foundations have been built and properly leveled, provide and lay all around, bearings or pieces to support the first floor beams, 3 x 8 or 3 x 10 inches, laid flatwise, and the outer edge either flush with the wall face, or back the thickness of the water-table. Halve and spike the bearings together at the angles, and where required to splice the pieces, lay the first floor beams of the required size, 16 inches from centers, from end to end of frame, starting the first floor beam the thickness of the first pair of corner studs from the end of the frame, and finishing out with a floor beam the same distance back from the face of the opposite end; secure all the beams on edge, by nailing into the bearings or sills, and nail in a course of bridging through the center of the tier. Now select a pair of studs for each floor beam, usually 3 x 4 inches, for intermediate, and 4 x 4 inches for corner studs, and long enough to reach from sills to plates, for $1\frac{1}{2}$, 2, or $2\frac{1}{2}$ story frames; higher than this they

would require splicing. The selection of studs
being made in pairs, one for each interval of
16 inches, saw them to a uniform length. Lay
off and cut a notch from the bottom up; the
height of the first story, and first story beams
large enough to receive a tie and bearing
piece 1 inch thick by 6 inches wide. Select
and cut the second floor beams to the required
length, "from out to out," one for each pair of
studs, and spike the beams to the studs, the
bottom of each beam to the top of the notches
and at right angles with the studs. Stay-lath
with diagonal braces. Then each pair of studs
and a floor beam will form a bent, which is
raised to a perpendicular position and nailed
at the bottom to the bearings or sills, and also
to the first floor beams; beginning at one end
of the frame, and raising successively a bent
or section (which was previously nailed together) for every space of 16 inches from
front to rear. Now plumb the front and rear
corner studs toward the gable ends of the
frame, and stay them. Prepare the 1 x 6 inch
tie, previously referred to, the proper length,

make the 16 inch spaces to correspond with those marked on the bearings or sills, and nail this tie into the notches prepared just under the second floor beams, adjusting the studs on both sides to their respective spaces. Nail in a course of bridging through the center of the second floor tier of beams. Provide and fix studs front and rear, or on each gable end. adjusting them to the required openings, and nailing to bearings at the bottom, and toe-nailing into the flat face of the outside floor beams front and rear, in the second story. Now provide and fix plate pieces 1 x 4 inches, or 1½ x 4, which we think better, nailing them in two thicknesses, or sections, to the top ends of the studs, in such a manner that the joints of the under piece will be covered or broken by the upper piece.

At this stage the frame in this system is considered raised, and the enclosing from the sills up to the plates is begun by cutting out the studs wherever an opening is required, and nailing in a header at the top and bottom, hanging the door and window frames, trimming the frame with water-table and corner boards, and laying the weather-boards.

Stair openings are cut through the floor beams wherever designated by the plan, and trimmed around with headers spiked to the ends. Rafters are fixed as in any ordinary frame.

A wood-cut, in "Woodward's Country Homes," by Geo. E. Woodward, illustrates, in an admirable manner, the important features in this system; and we refer such of our readers as require additional information, respecting balloon frames, to that and the accompanying chapter.

### THE EXTERNAL COVERING OF FRAMES.

In the remarks preceding, we have briefly described the manner of building various frames, or those parts of the wooden wall that support the floors and roof of a building. A finished wall includes an external covering, and in some cases a "filling in" between the studs of brick, plaster, or concrete. The covering most common for all frame dwellings is clap-

4*

boards, $\frac{1}{2}$ inch thick by 5 and 6 inches wide, with the upper edge slightly beveled, so as to insure a close fitting lap. These, as nearly every one knows, are laid and nailed to the vertical studs of the frame horizontally, with a uniform lap of $\frac{3}{4}$ to $1\frac{1}{4}$ inches. To insure additional strength, and some additional warmth, the outside of the frame is sheathed diagonally with 1 inch boards, and upon these the clapboards, or weather-boards, are laid. To secure some degrees more of warmth, either fill in between the studs with brick, on edge, laid with close joints in lime mortar, back plaster between the studs, fill in with concrete, shingle the sides O. S. over the sheathing, or lay tared paper, or felt, well lapped on the sheathing before laying the weather-boards.

These modes are applicable to the balloon, as well as the skeleton, or mortise and tenon frame, and we consider sheathing essential in either; for the purpose of strengthening the frame where there are perpendicular studs, the sheathing should be applied diagonally at an angle of 30°, in continuous courses, from one corner to another all around the building, breaking joints alternately. We have seen the diagonal method applied with the angle reversed on one half of the side and a perpendicular joint run up through the middle; this may be considered a constructive fallacy, as the object of diagonal sheathing is to prevent, as much as possible, spreading the laps of weather-boards, that sheathing applied horizontally might occasion. In point of strength the horizontal sheathing is best.

Vertical boarding is another mode of covering, and when required, either the mortise and tenon, or balloon frame can be prepared for it. The former will require story posts, or studs, at the openings, and a series of horizontal girths, about 3 feet apart from the sills up, framed into the posts. The girths for ordinary buildings should be 3 x 5 inches, and posts 4 x 6 inches, allowing for an inch furring, nailed 16 inches from centers to the girths to receive the lath and plaster; this gives a wall equal in strength and thickness to the regularly framed wall.

To provide for this covering in the balloon frame, we cut and nail in, rows of horizontal bridging, 3 feet apart, from sills to plates, using wall strips or other light yard timber, and without disturbing, or otherwise changing the mode. Vertical boarding is seldom applied unless designed as a finish for the exterior, in which case it should be narrow, mill-worked or matched, and thoroughly seasoned, accompanied with the proper trimmings, and if joints are to be battened, the boards should not be under 6 inches, or exceed 7 inches, in width. If no battens, the boards should not exceed 3 inches in width.

The external covering sometimes consists of plain ceiling laid horizontally, and when such is the design, the boards should be tongued and grooved, not over 3 inches wide ; and it is important for the exclusion of wet, that in laying them, the tongues should appear on the upper edge, and the grooved edge of each course be driven down over it. In either mode, the boards should be principally "blind nailed."

Frames are frequently "filled in" between
the studs, between the outer and inner coverings, to close as many of the crevices in the
outer wall as possible, and thus provide a
warmer dwelling. The usual methods resort-
ed to for securing this end, are, the brick on
edge, concrete filling, back-plastering, and the
application of tared paper well lapped on the
outside of the sheathing. If a frame is not to
be sheathed, it should be filled in with brick
or concrete, (brick is the least expensive,) as
it is thereby steadied and enabled to oppose
weight, to force of winds in lieu of the
strength obtained by sheathing. If sheathing
is employed, either back-plaster—as the frame
would be sufficiently stiff in this case to allow
of it—or cover the sheathing with a double
thickness of tared paper, which mode is now
greatly preferred, on account of the elasticity
of the paper and the perfect manner in which
it keeps out wind and rain.

### THE ROOF.

The roof is the most important part of a dwelling. Its design is to afford protection, to give character, and determine the quality of the building, besides rendering it attractive as an architectural composition or design; and as the terminal feature of the building, it requires to be accurately balanced to every requirement of style and utility.

Modern roofs are now constructed in a great variety of forms, which indicate the license allowed to fancy as well as judgment and taste. Although we have departed from the systematic arrangement of the ancients, in regard to some portions of the roof, we are still able to employ their classifications for other, and more prominent parts, upon which its strength and character depends, as illustrated by the following:

*Trabes*—Wall plate or beam.

*Culmen*—Ridge pole.

*Columen*—King post.

*Transtræ*—Principal rafters.

*Capreoli*—Struts and braces.

*Canterii*—Common rafters.

*Templa*—Pole plates and purlins.

The above terms designate parts of the simpler form of span, or pediment roof, for narrow spans.     Broad spans require a composite truss, introducing the queen post, straining sill and beam, (tabled and bolted,) and additional studs and braces.     They are also applied to such parts of the hip-roof, truncated, French, or revolved roof, as have a similar place in the construction.

The styles of roof with which American builders are most familiarly acquainted are,

The Span roof, double and single, Grecian and Gothic pitch.

The Bell cast roof.

The Truncated roof.

The Hipped roof.

The French, or Mansard, and curbed roof.

The flat roof.

These styles are all employed in our northern latitudes at varying angles of inclination to the horizon (according to the materials employed to cover them) from 4° to 70°.

Those pitches which have become standard in the styles of architecture, are the Grecian, requiring an inclination of 12° to 16°; the Roman, 22° to 24°; the Gothic, 45° to 60°; and the Elizabethan, 60° to 70°. Roofs covered with tin, concrete, or gravel, require a pitch of 4°. Slates, shingles, or tiles, require a pitch not less than $22\frac{1}{2}$°, and may be suitably employed on any pitch from this, to 60°.

Scantlings for the roof should be as nearly proportioned as possible to the weight of the material used for covering, and where the roof has the elements of the double span, whether the pitch be high or low, these may be accurately approximated by the rules in Sec. 4 of "Tredgold's Principles of Carpentry."

The following is a tabular exhibit of the comparative weight of various coverings to the square, according to the degrees of inclination to the horizon :

| *Materials.* | *Inclination.* | *Weight.* |
|---|---|---|
| Galvanized Iron, wire gauge, No. 23, | 4 degs | .........125 lbs. |
| Tin, Leaded, IC, ................... | 4 " | ......... 56 " |
| Tin, Leaded, IK, ................... | 4 " | ......... 70 " |
| Slates, ordinary, thick American, 26 to 30 | " | ..300 to 500 " |
| Slates, American Stone, ........26 to 30 | " | .......2380 " |
| Slates, large Welsh, . ..........26 to 30 | " | .......1120 " |
| Shingles, . ......... ..........26 to 30 | " | ......... 60 " |
| Gravel Roofing, ............... 4 to 8 | " | .........600 " |
| Corrugated Iron, ............. 4 to 22½ | " | .........600 " |

For low pitched roofs and flats, gravel is sometimes used with the tared paper and melted pitch, the application of which need not be described as it is so well known.

Tin is a reliable and standard covering, and better than any other material for a low pitch, except corrugated iron. For roofing purposes, lead plates, the brand I C or I K, should be always used. The latter is better, because heavier. Tin is often laid upon rough hemlock or wide mill-worked boards, but a better roof is made by having the tin underlaid with narrow mill-worked boards. Roof gutters, valleys and flashings should be laid of the same quality of lead plate, and painted on the under sides before being laid down. All tin work should be painted on the outside two or three good coats with french ochre and linseed oil, gray or slate color, or to harmonize with the general tint of the building. For leaders, the brands D C, to D X X X X, and brands C I I W, to X I I W, are best. For slates, the roof may be "covered in" with rough boards laid edge to edge, but should invariably be covered under the slates with a double thickness of tared paper, or felt well lapped, to prevent drift from sifting into the attic, or a driving storm from wetting the ceiling. A lap of 3 inches should be given to all slates, and if varied from, should exceed this measure at the eaves, and diminish toward the ridge. The pitch for slates should never be less than one fourth ($\frac{1}{4}$) the span or width of roof. Valleys should be one to two-thirds broader for slates than for other ordinary coverings. Slates are sometimes laid upon laths or parallel pieces $1\frac{1}{4}$ x 3 inches; this method will do very well for a steep pitch if well pointed with mortar back of each course on the inside of the roof.

They are also laid upon mill-worked boards without being underlaid with any material to prevent drift—a practice not safe, or advisable, with ordinary American slates. There are twenty one sizes of slates, from 14 x 7 to 24 x 16 inches; averaging from 3-16 to 5-16 of an inch in thickness. Of foreign, or Welsh slates, there are thirteen sizes, from 13 x 6 to 36 x 24 inches. For beauty and cleanliness, slates are unsurpassed as a roof covering; they give a dwelling character and dignity, especially if it be wood, and the roof a certain imperishable look, which is here desirable over all other parts of the building. They require, however, to be laid with the greatest care to insure a weather-tight roof.

Shingles of pine, cedar, or cypress are much used; some oak and butternut shingles are used where these woods are more plentiful and easier obtained than pine. Shingles are laid much as slates are, and upon rough roof boards or shingle laths. It is not necessary to lay them upon mill-worked boards, or to underlay them with tared paper, or any other material, to obtain a weather-tight roof. Shingles are sawed, cut, and shaved; the sawed and cut will lay, and form a tighter roof than the shaved, while the latter will probably endure the longest, because the surfaces, although uneven, are smooth, and the grain in a parallel direction. Shingles are usually cut in lengths of 15 and 18 inches, and in widths of from 2 to 10 inches. The former length requires a lap of 4 inches, or should lay $5\frac{1}{2}$ inches to the weather. The latter should lap 5 inches, and lay $6\frac{1}{2}$ inches to the weather, and in all cases the joints should not be "broken" at a less distance apart than 1 inch. They should not be employed upon any pitch designed for dwellings under 20°, but should exceed it if possible.

### TIMBER—ITS PROPERTIES AND PRESERVATION.

To employ timber advantageously, requires an intellegent understanding of its nature and properties, and, therefore, for economical uses, we should know how trees are affected by their geographical situation, by soil, growth, change of organs, and disease.

Trees, termed by botanists dicotyledonous plants, with respect to their wood, may be divided into three classes—the hard, soft, and the resinous woods. In the first, we have the Oak, Beech, Apple, Chestnut, Ash, Elm, Mahogany, and Black-Walnut. The second comprises the Willow, White Wood, American White or Northern Pine, and Cedar. And the third, White and Yellow Fir, Larch, American Yellow, or Southern Pine.

In the germination and growth of the Dicotyledonous, or woody plants, the vascular system begins to organize around the pith and to form medullary rays, whose extremities exhibit cellular texture, which is soon formed into libers. The libers expand, then harden, and are in a short time converted into a layer of alburnum. The alburnum gradually acquires tenacity and hardness, until perfect wood is the result. Meanwhile the cambium, or sap, (which is a cellular mass flowing between the bark and the wood,) hardens into a new layer of liber, which again merging into alburnum, and then perfect wood; other layers succeed until the growth is stopped.

Each layer is the product of one year's growth, so that if a tree should be cut transversely at the base, or near the ground, its age could generally be determined by the annual rings. While the circumference of the tree is being yearly expanded, it also grows higher each year in exact ratio: the rings gradually disappearing at the top of the tree, until the extremities of the branches contain the continuation of but one annual layer. Botanical science informs us how the height of a tree is produced. At the germination of the seed, the plume rises, and the liber is developed by the vegetative power and made to grow upward, developing gradually, and extending less, until it is converted into wood, when it ceases growing. This new layer of wood resembles an elongated cone, upon which a bud is formed and from which a new shoot starts. A new liber is here formed, which in turn becomes woody fiber, increasing the diameter and height of a tree each successive year. If we were to cut a transverse section of oak, chestnut, ash, or elm, the annual growth could be distinctly traced with the grains partly compact and partly porous, while beech, mahogany, and black-walnut would present nearly a uniform texture, with indistinct markings of their annual growth. The soft and resinous woods would also be, more or less, distinctly marked by annual rings of variegated color, a part hard, and a part soft. The resinous would be particularly distinguished by the pores of the wood filled with pitch. A clayey or calcarous soil produces most of our hard woods, and a quartzose soil, the resinous and soft woods, with some two or three species of the hard, as red and white oak black-walnut, and chestnut.

THE OAK—(*Quercus*), is regarded as the most durable, the strongest, and toughest of all woods. In a dry state, and where the grain is compact and close, it has been known to last for more than a thousand years. Buried in the earth, it will last, relatively speaking, forever, and in water will resist disease and decay for an extremely long period.    The American species are the red, white, iron, and chestnut-leaved; of these, the white and iron oaks are the most durable. They are all slightly astringent to the taste and contain gallic acid, and in seasoning warp and twist. When thoroughly seasoned, they diminish about one to three per cent in bulk.

THE BEECH—*( Fagus )*, has a close and solid grain, but is not durable in either damp or dry situations, and unless used where it can lay immersed in water, or quite excluded from the air, as for mud-sills or piles, should not be employed generally for building purposes. To protect it from the incursions of worms, it should be cut in midsummer and laid a few days in water. This wood will also warp considerably, but after seasoning, will not shrink much.

THE CHESTNUT—*( Castanea vesca )*, is a coarse grained, dark, sienna colored wood, resembling oak, and useful for the same purposes, but at maturity not as tough or stiff.    It attains to considerable size in a quartzose soil, and in a mean annual temperature of about 50°.

For posts to place in the ground, or timbers to sustain weight, vertically or horizontally, select young timber, which is tough and flexible. Old chestnut is brittle and not to be depended upon for such a purpose. It may be used for interior finishings for dwellings, either with or without other woods, and will not shrink and swell as much as oak.

THE ASH—*(Fraxinus)*, is quite tough and elastic when not very old. Our common American species are the (acuminate) white and black ash. The former is valuable for many purposes, and used by builders for floors and interior finishings, and by wheel and mill-wrights. The latter species is not considered valuable, and is seldom employed. Exposed alternately to a wet and dry atmosphere, they decay rapidly. White ash does not warp as much as oak; texture is compact and porus alternately —a rapid grower.

THE ELM—*(Ulmus Americana)*, or white

5

elm, is a tough, cross and coarse grained wood, used very little for building, excellent and very durable for pile timbers, docking, &c.     Heart-wood, dark ; sap-wood, whitish brown ; warps badly, and shrinks end and width-wise.     The branches of the tree are smooth, leaves oblique at the base, having acuminate serratures.

*Ulmus Pendula,* is a weeping tree with hanging branches and smooth leaves, and propagated by nurserymen, as an ornamental deciduous tree.

*Ulmus Fulva,* Slippery Elm, is a species commonly found in a calcerous soil.     The branches are scabrous and white, leaves ovate, oblong, very acuminate.     The inner bark, or cortex, furnishes a mucilage that is medicinal.

MAHOGANY—*(Swietenia Mahogani.)*     This tree is a native of the Torrid Zone, and imported in large quanties, in the log, from the West Indies and Bay of Honduras.     The former is commonly known as Spanish, or Saint Domingo mahogany.     The grain is close and hard, and color, dark red brown.     The latter,

known as the "Bay Wood" mahogany, is
coarse grained, of larger growth, beautifully
veined, and sometimes mottled.   Leaves of
the tree are lanceolate-ovate, acuminate ;
racems axillary, downy.   Mahogany is extensively used for the interior finish of buildings,
panels, stair rails and balusters, doors, wainscot, and architraves, and for cabinet ware,
furniture, &c.

W ALNUT—*(Juglans Alba.)*   White walnut,
or hickory tree, is tough and flexible, quite
durable, if kept dry.   In large trees the sap-
wood is white and hard, the heart-wood, light
red, or brown.   Employed but little for building purposes, but used by wheel-wrights, and
cut into cord wood for winter fuel.   Saplings
are used, on account of their toughness, for
splint-brooms, ax-helves, hand-spikes, &c.

*Juglans Nigra*, or Black Walnut, is a large
tree, the wood dark, or umber colored, close
grained, tough in young trees, brittle in old
ones.   Sometimes beautifully mottled ; employed for the same purposes as mahogany
and quite as durable, and unlike the white

walnut, not affected by worms. This species is found in the north, the western, and southern states in abundance, and is one of our most valuable woods for economical uses and for the interior finish of buildings. Large quantities are annually used in the manufacture of every style of furniture, plain and antique.

WHITE PINE, or Weymouth North American pine—(*Pinus Strobus*), is a wood more extensively used for the frame work and finish of dwellings than any other. This wood is light and soft, and its specific gravity about 4·60; the color, after exposure, becomes dark yellow; when first worked it is a light buff or straw color. The texture is uniform, and the annual rings indistinct. Is much used for doors, sashes, blinds, and shutters; interior finish of all kinds; masts and cabins of vessels, floors, timbers, and moulds; not so durable as yellow pine when exposed to the weather unpainted, or unprotected by a chemical solution.

*Pinus Resinosa*, or yellow pine, is grown, and most abundant, in southern latitudes, and hence called southern pine and sometimes

Georgia pine, from the large quantities brought from the State of Georgia northward ; the color is brownish yellow, distinctly veined, texture hard, and pores filled with an oily resin ; very durable.

The leaves and sheaths of the tree are elongated, strobiles ovate-conic, rounded at the base, scales dilated in the middle. Grows tall and straight, with redish bark ; smoother than the white pine.

The other American species, are the

*Pinus Rigida,* or Pitch Pine, common in barren and sandy soils.

*Pinus Eanadensis,* or Hemlock tree.

*Pinus Balsamea,* or American silver, and balsam fir.

*Pinus Pendula,* or Blk Larch, and Tamarack, whose leaves are deciduous.

### SELECTION OF TREES FOR TIMBER, ETC.

The best season for selecting trees to cut for timber is midsummer, at which time the foliage in healthy trees is full and dark green ; while trees diseased in any way, have a somewhat variegated foliage, with the trunks often moss and ivy grown.

Trees on the decline, furnish a brittle, or brash wood, while those that have arrived at maturity, furnish durable and tough timber for every purpose. Saplings, or young trees, do not furnish durable and stiff timber, and should not be cut for this purpose.

To secure the trees selected, they may be marked by girdling, and so hasten the seasoning of the timber, as this process severs the outer bark and liber, and prevents the flow of the cambium, or sap; but trees in this condition should not be left standing too long, lest, after the decline of the tree in this way, it should become affected with dry rot, or worms.

### SEASONING AND PRESERVATION OF TIMBER.

Freshly cut timber contains from 40 to 50 per cent of vegetable juices, or sap, which becomes solidified when completely dry; and when only partially seasoned, as by the ordinary method of piling in tiers, it retains about

20 per cent of juices, or moisture; and when thoroughly seasoned, about 10 per cent of moisture is said yet to remain. Two to six years are required to perfectly season timber.

Timber seasoned by a slow and gradual process in the atmosphere, is most durable; and that which is charred or painted, in a green state, is quickly destroyed by fermentation and decay.

Dry rot is infused into timber by exposure to wet and dry alternately; hence the timbers of frames should be "covered in," or protected from the weather.

Timber may be very much improved, its texture hardened, and its durability increased, by boiling or steaming it. It may be permanently protected from wet or dry rot, the adherence of animal or vegetable parasites, or attacks of insects, by being impregnated with either a solution of *corrosive sublimate, chloride of zinc,* or *sulphate of copper.* The use of chloride of zinc, in the process patented by Sir William Burnett, is probably the most safe and economical, and is called "Burnettizing," and consists of a solution of 1℔ of chloride to 10 gallons of water, submitted to the wood or timber end-wise, under a pressure of 130 to 150 ℔s to the square inch. By this process wood may be rendered uninflammable ; and as the solution enters into perfect chemical combination with the ligneous fiber, efflorescence does not take place, and continued bleaching and boiling will not remove the solution, or impair its virtue in the least.

Below we give a tabular view of the comparative weight, stiffness, strength, and toughness of the preceding species.

| Kind of Wood. | Weight of cub. ft. | Stiffness. | Strength. | Toughness. |
|---|---|---|---|---|
| Oak, W. A., | 56 | 114 | 86 | 64 |
| Beech, | 53 | 77 | 100 | 130 |
| Chestnut, | 43 | 67 | 89 | 118 |
| Ash, | 52 | 89 | 119 | 160 |
| Elm, | | 78 | 82 | 86 |
| Mahogany, Hond., | | 93 | 96 | 99 |
| Black Walnut, | | 50 | 78 | 100 |
| White, Pine, | 28 | 95 | 99 | 103 |
| Yellow, " Va., | 34,2 | 100 | 105 | 95 |
| Pitch, " | 41 | 73 | 82 | 92 |

## PAINTING.

Painting, employed as a vehicle of use and ornament about our dwellings, deserves greater consideration than is usually given to it. Excessive haste is too often manifested in the selection and use of colors, at the sacrifice of durability and proper effect; whereas a little thoughtfulness, and a few well-directed inquiries would have spared many a one the humiliating sense of incompleteness in their own efforts and works. Accepting this as a fact, I have believed, and do still, that it is not a knowledge of what ought to be done we want so much as a frequent reminding of our duty toward impressions and materials.

I am sometimes asked, "How would you perform this or that piece of house painting, so as to insure reasonable durability with proper tones of color?" and have answered in general terms, that it is only required, as a first rule, to observe what *are* good materials; and secondly, how they should be applied.

When any are sought. it should be determined first what are best, since the best are cheapest, though double or treble the cost of inferior ones at the outset, because of greater facility in working them, their excellence of finish, and lasting qualities.

White lead is used as a base for nearly all the positive and semi-tones in house painting, and is best when old, because it is thus rendered softer and finer, and works smoothly under the brush. The unadulterated keg-lead should be used for good work. Its preparation in detail I will not attempt; but may remark, that it is sometimes prepared by exposing sheet-lead to the fumes of vinegar, by which it is corroded, and its surface covered with an incrustation, which being scraped off and levigated, becomes white lead. It is again made by precipitating a solution of acetate of lead by carbonate of soda, consisting of about 112 oxide of lead, and 22 carbonic acid, etc. Semitones are compounded from white as a base, and some of the varieties of the other primitive colors, black, red, yellow, blue, green, and brown. Of the four or more varieties of black, lampblack calcined and ground in boiled linseed oil is probably the best for general purposes.

Of thirteen varieties of red, Carmine and Indian, Chinese and English pale vermillions, Orange Mineral and Prussian Red are most reliable for wood-work, though nearly all the kinds are in use constantly.

Of the several varieties of yellow, Chinese and French Ochre are the best; the former clear, enduring, and of great strength; the latter takes but little oil, and preserves its color well.

Of the blues, Ultramarine, Chinese, Prussian, and Antwerp are the best, being of great strength, and easily ground in oil.

Out of the greens, I select Chrome and Paris greens. Both should be ground fine in boiled linseed oil, and used on carefully prepared priming.

All the varieties of brown are quite good. and freely used in the various branches of house painting and decorating, but chiefly to prepare drabs, and for veining imitations of wood.

In the application of the materials for painting, a hint or two, enjoining the workman to pay due regard to the small things of his craft, will not be out of place ; and the practical experience of a most excellent master painter, teaches that this is positively necessary to give any thing like a satisfactory result.   Brushes and vessels must be kept clean ; and no good workman will be without a proper number of these.   Pots for colors, cans for oils and turpentines, and tin paint-pots, from which the colors are used with the brush.   Marble slab and muller for grinding colors, or pigments. Large ground brush, pound brush, half size. Duster, pallet, and putty-knife, sash-tools, ladders and window-jack.   Strong tin cans for using the paint from is better than wooden ones, because easily kept clean and brushed down ; paint can not adhere to these so well, and hence less is wasted.   Prepare the wood work for painting by first examining to see if any roughness of surface is apparent, caused by working against the grain of the wood, or from any other cause; if so, destroy the roughness, and level the irregularities by a liberal use of sand-paper, assorted, and pumice. This should be done before the priming coat of paint is spread, or put on, and not afterward, as is sometimes the case, since the priming aids in forming the body, and is nearly all taken up by the pores of the wood, and consequently would be nearly all removed from the surface in preparing for the after coats of painting.

All wood work, whether out or indoor, (excepting it be well worked hard wood,) comes to the painter in a comparatively rough state; the finished surface is either glassy or wooley, mottled or ridgy, according to the direction of the grain, the quality of the wood used, and the manner, or way, in which the several pieces forming the finish were treated by the workman.

Puttying may always be done after the priming has set or dried, but knotting and shellacing should be thoroughly done before priming. All spots of sap-wood, and those impregnated with pitch, should receive two coats of size to prevent their defects being seen through the finishing coats.

In white painting this precaution is not to be omitted, if we would have a pure white instead of a dirty yellow. The discoloration of white paint, so frequently seen, is, however, not always due to the imperfect preparation of the wood, but sometimes white painting is caused to assume a yellow tinge by the withdrawal of light from apartments.

Where fast knots appear they should be covered with two coats of size; if loose or black, should be bored out and plugged. All knots, however, should be avoided on the interior finish of first class buildings, on account of the difficulty of completely covering them, with even the best care.

There seems a difference of opinion as to the number of coats required for plain work in the first painting; but when it is remembered that the priming coat is nearly all taken in by absorption, it will be seen that not less than three coats will suffice for white, and two coats for neutral tints. For new outside work, this will be found sufficient for about the first three years; after which there will need to be a renewal, since its vitality and power to resist the wear of weather becomes partially destroyed.

Inside painting being employed as a vehicle of ornament as much as for the preservation of wood work, its restoration, or renewal, is more subject to the rules of taste than any absolute requirement of utility, though, if well done, it would serve all purposes by being renewed, or restored, every three or five years.

In performing the necessary manipulations for house painting, the priming coats for exterior work should be mixed with clear old white lead and pure linseed oil, in about the proportion of ten pounds of white lead for every two quarts of oil. For interior painting, it is best to use with the lead boiled linseed oil exclusively, instead of raw, or a proportion of boiled and raw, as is sometimes done, with a small quantity of patent dryer, ground in turpentine, which will cause the priming to set quick and form a body without dripping.  For exterior second coat work, use the priming process, and add thereto sufficient white lead to make the paint quite stiff.    If neutral tints are used, then estimate about two-thirds of the above proportion of lead to be added to one-half its bulk of color, and all the oil they will take.   This, as a general rule, and for common use, is sufficient.   But as there are several degrees of strength, of fineness, and of quality in colors, so there must be many rules, or rather no definite rules at all; only, artist-like, a conception of what is demanded, and a constant working with muller, paint, and brush, until it is answered in the very tone and impression sought.    For second coating interior work, grind the white lead in raw linseed oil to the consistency of thick paste ; then reduce it with turpentine until in a proper condition to spread with the brush, using, as a general rule, an equal quantity of oil and turpentine, to complete the mixing process.    The second may sometimes be made a finishing coat by the addition of a larger proportion of turpentine, and by straining the color carefully, and adding a portion of the finest French zinc, equal in proportion to half the quantity of lead used, supposing the finish to be a clear dead white.

For neutral tints, the addition of the required color in the proper proportions to the white, mixed as above, for a base, is sufficient. I would not, unless in some exceptional cases, advise the use of two coat work for completely finishing the wood work, but wish to be understood as urging the necessity of not stopping short of good *three* coat work, and in some cases four and five coat work.

In preparing the third coat, if designed for a dead white, the ingredients should be, first, equal parts of the best old American white lead, and the best quality of French zinc, ground in equal parts of raw linseed oil and turpentine, as stiff as possible, and afterwards reduced with all turpentine to the proper consistency for use.

If it should be required to finish with a superior gloss, (technically termed China gloss,) then the work must receive a coat of white shellac upon the priming, and the last or third coat should be composed of three parts zinc to one of lead, ground in oil and turpentine, and reduced with the latter, and after becoming dry should have, in addition, one coat of the best white varnish, and to perfect the gloss, add still another coat.

An exceedingly beautiful white paint for interior wood work may be obtained by the following process: To one half gallon of turpentine add twenty ounces of frankincense; place it over a fire to dissolve, after which strain and put in cans for use. To one quart of this mixture add three quarts of bleached linseed oil. To these two mixtures combined, add equal parts of clear old white lead and the best French zinc, ground in turpentine. Strain them; and if too stiff, reduce with turpentine, as for other interior work. Paint prepared in this manner gives out scarcely any odor, and if well done, will preserve its fine finish many years; but its great cost, compared with the commoner kinds of white paint, prevents it coming into general use.

*Graining.*—If we were disposed, and could always accept the conditions of procuring and preparing the better class of woods for house finishing, it would be better to do so, on account of their real and undisguised worth, and the consideration in which they are held in all true architecture ; but in the absence of an abundance of the rarer and finer woods, as walnut, oak, cherry, rosewood, maple, and mahogany, graining in imitation of these has seemed to become, in these days of rapid building, highly proper, and an almost universal vehicle of covering for soft wood finish, and for ornament ; and since it is thus thought to be rarely possible, and seldom expedient, to employ woods richly veined, and susceptible of oil and polish, there exist suitable reasons for grained imitations, when we know and accept them as such ; the same as we would use gilding in the absence or scarcity of gold, or stucco ornaments instead of, and to represent, carvings in marble.

Graining may be properly employed in nearly all branches of domestic architecture, but should never intrude in the higher fields of civil and ecclesiastical architecture.

It may be employed upon the wood work of dining-rooms of a cheerful oak imitation, on walls, saloons, and lobbies, either in oak or walnut. In libraries, in imitation of English walnut, rosewood, or old oak. Bed-chambers and closets should never be painted white, but be grained in imitation of chestnut or pollard oak, whose tones are quiet and subdued, without glare or reflected lights. Kitchens and kitchen offices may be grained in imitation of either oak, maple, or chestnut, provided it be finished in oil, and not varnished ; otherwise a flatting of good warm drab or French gray, on two coats of priming, with lead and oil, will be found both serviceable and easily kept clean.

A good piece of grained work, like any other work, derives its chief excellence from good and proper materials and skillful handling ; and to answer fully this last demand, it is required that the artist or grainer study closely the character and grains of the woods to be imitated, and also enter into an analysis of them all. But I desire to afford the reader facilities for judging of, and selecting good materials for graining, (if he does not already know,) and hence shall repeat the process as briefly as possible for some of the best grains in modern use.

*Oak.*—To prepare a rich ground for oak graining, take old white lead, three parts; burnt terra sienna, three parts; stone ochre, two parts; chrome yellow, one; put on two coats, and when dry apply the graining color, composed of raw terra sienna, Vandyke brown, and whiting in about equal portions ground in oil or beer; add about four ounces of gum Arabic, dissolved in a pint of hot water. Mix it well with the other ingredients, and when perfectly dry, varnish with two coats of copal varnish.

*Old Oak.*—To imitate old oak, make a ground of about equal parts of stone ochre and burnt terra sienna, with one part lead ground in oil. Put on in two coats, and pre-pare the graining color either of burnt umber

or Vandyke brown mixed in oil.   Another
method, which I think superior to the last for
old oak *grain color*, is to grind Vandyke brown
and whiting in turpentine, and add a small
quantity of common soap to make it stand the
comb.

*Pollard Oak.*—A species of graining used
considerably in England, and more mottled
than common oak, may be imitated by preparing a ground of chrome yellow three parts,
vermillion one, white lead three; when mixed
the result will be a rich buff.   The graining
colors are prepared from equal parts of Tur-
key umber, raw terra sienna, and burnt white
vitriol, ground separately in oil to the consistency of paste, and reduced with turpentine,
taking care, however, to keep a sufficient
quantity of oil in the colors to bind and finish
well.

*Mahogany Grounds*, may be prepared in the
following manner.: To twelve or fourteen
ounces of English Venetian red, add three
ounces of chrome yellow, and one ounce of
vermilion, ground in equal portions of oil and

turpentine. This ground must be applied to the wood in two coats, upon a priming of lead and oil, quite stiff, stained with a little red lead. The graining color may be prepared with raw and burnt terra sienna, in equal parts, ground in ale. To imitate mahogany more perfectly, there may be a top grain prepared of burnt sienna, and applied after the first grain color has been worked with mottler and softener, and become perfectly dry.

*Rosewood*, may be imitated by preparing for a ground with one part white lead, one part crimson lake, and two parts vermilion, ground in oil, and put on in two coats. The graining color is prepared of Vandyke brown, ground in oil quite thin, with a darker after-tint of the same kind of color, to be used with the graining brush, to soften and draw the more delicate veins over the work. When dry, apply two coats of varnish, reduced, if need be, with alcohol, to preserve its gloss.

*Neutral Tints.*—And now that enough has been said about graining to enable the reader to form a pretty correct estimate of what

materials are good, and what should be used,
I propose to give some directions for the preparation of *neutral tints*, as well as inquire into
some of the leading principles that ought to
govern their production, principally for exterior house painting.

I presume the term "neutral tints" is well
enough understood theoretically, though its
practical modern signification be not fully
comprehended.   In connection with house
painting, it does not mean any one of the positive colors, as white, black, red, blue, etc.,
nor a single compound of some particular and
specified *two* positives, producing a specified
color ; but such a use and combination of positive colors as will produce, in harmony and
variety, any and all the intermediate tones
from white to black.   Color may be divided
into three classes ; Primary, consisting of red,
blue, or yellow ; Secondary, produced by mixing two primaries ; Tertiary, produced by
mixing two secondaries.   Harmony of color is
two-fold, by analogy, and by contrast.   Those
tones are most perfectly neutral, or harmoni-

ous, that are made to possess the most relative harmony without striking contrast.

When two or more tones are employed on one separate subject, as in the case of particolored painting for trimmings and the body of the building, they should harmonize, with only perceptible difference enough to make them distinguishable.

The harmony of colors by contrast may be stated, as a general principle, in the following manner :

1. Red harmonizes with orange or yellow, though positive in tone.

2. Orange harmonizes with drab.

3. Yellow harmonizes with white.

4. Green harmonizes with yellow.

5. Blue harmonizes with white and red.

6. Brown harmonizes with green and black.

But in the production of neutral tints they may be better exemplified in the following practical methods :

1st. *Cream Color* is produced by using equal parts of white and red lead, English Venetian red one part, chrome yellow two parts, ground in oil. *Free Stone* color harmonizes with this, and is produced with red lead as a principal ingredient, English Venetian red one part, lampblack one part, and French yellow two parts, ground in oil and turpentine.

2d. *Drab* is produced with white lead, French yellow, and lampblack, ground in three parts oil and one of turpentine. *Orange* harmonizes with drab, and may be produced of a pleasing tint with French and chrome yellow, equal parts, half the quantity of white and red lead, ground in oil.

3d. *Fawn Color.* Reduce raw terra sienna to powder, and use one pound to fifty pounds of white lead ground in oil. A beautiful warm *Drab* to harmonize with this may be prepared with white lead two and a half parts, burnt umber one and a half parts, raw terra sienna half part, and enough of the best English Venetian red to stain the colors and impart a warm hue.

4th. *French Gray*, of a superior quality and color, may be produced with white lead three parts, Prussian blue one part, vermilion half part, burnt terra sienna quarter part, ground in oil and a small portion of turpentine. Substitute carmine for vermilion in the last coat. *Straw Color* harmonizes with the above, and may be produced with white lead three parts, chrome yellow one part, ground in three parts oil and one part turpentine. *Buff*, also, will harmonize with French gray, it being nearly the same as straw color, and is prepared with white lead four parts, French and chrome yellows two parts each, and one part red lead.

5th. *Pearl Gray*, is produced with white lead and equal parts of Prussian blue and lampblack, mixed in oil. *Free Stone* harmonizes with this, and is usually produced with red lead as a principal ingredient, and English Venetian red one part, lampblack one part, and French yellow two parts, ground in oil and turpentine. To lighten the tint, a small quantity of white lead may be used.

6th. Another good *Fawn Color* may be produced with white lead as a base, and equal parts of vermilion or carmine, and stone ochre, ground in oil. *Pearl Gray* does well with this also, prepared as specified in the 5th section.

7th. To prepare a pleasing *Chestnut Color*, mix stone yellow, vermilion, and black, using white lead as a base, ground in oil. *Chocolate Color* harmonizes with this, and may be produced with white lead three parts, common Venetian red two parts, red lead one part, and black one part, ground in boiled linseed oil, to harden the color.

8th. A good *Stone Color* may be produced with white lead as a base, and equal parts of burnt umber and yellow ochre. *Fawn Color*, as specified in section 6th, does well with this.

I have now extended my remarks upon the subject of house painting far enough, I trust, to make the attentive reader quite familiar with some of its best materials, and the best methods for employing them ; and where the proportions have been given, they may be taken for as safe and proper rules as can probably be ever attained to in a branch of art whose governing law is taste rather than rule.

## Design One.

## PICTURESQUE STONE COTTAGE.

———◦◦⚬⚬◦◦———

BEAUTY of outline and proportion is as important in the design and construction of a house, as the interior arrangement of the dwelling. A "square box' may afford all necessary facilities to the family, but if it does not please the eye and gratify the esthetic as well as the animal wants, it lacks an indispensable part of what a fine country house ought to be. The large number of houses which have been put up during the last three or four years on the great thoroughfares of travel leading out of New York, have afforded a good opportunity for the exercise of the talents of our Architects, and the

Fig. 1.

skill of our suburban Builders. The design
we give (No. 1) was executed of stone, at
" Highwood Park," Tenafly Station, on the line
of the Northern New Jersey Rail Road, and
situate on the western Palisade slope.

### ARRANGEMENT.

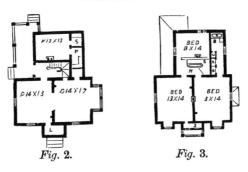

*Fig.* 2.        *Fig.* 3.

Fig. 1, is a perspective view, and Figs. 2
and 3 are first and second floor plans. The
style is a modification of the Gothic, with
"bell-cast" roof. The main building is 17 x 30
feet, and the extension 20 x 21 feet. The whole,
two stories and attic, with a cellar and a basement kitchen below. Exposure, south-wester-
ly. The first floor, Fig. 2, contains: L, lobby,
5 x 8 feet; P, parlor, $13\frac{1}{2}$ x 14 feet; D, dining-

room, 14 x 17½ feet; H, open hall and stair-case; K, kitchen, 13 x 14 feet, besides sink-room, pantry and china-closet. Fig. 3, is the second floor plan, containing three sleeping rooms, 13 x 14 feet; a bath-room, 6 x 10 feet, with a passage for communication from front to rear rooms, and wardrobe at the side; *c, c,* are closets. The attic contains space for four rooms, about 8 x 10 and 12 feet. The parlor and dining room are separated by folding doors, and may be *en suite* when required; and are warmed, with the chambers above them, by the furnace.

*Cost.*—The cost of the house, including a well, entrance gates, grading and walks, will not exceed $6,000. The following are the principal items of cost. The walls, the most costly item, were laid up in random courses of silicious, or sand stone, white and red, and contain about—

5,000 cubic feet of stone work at 30c., . . . . . . . . . . . . $1,500 00
    (This includes pointing and excavation for cellar.)
8,000 feet timber and rough lumber at 24-00, . . . . . .   192 00
Shingles, lath, flooring, finishing pine, architraves
  and moulds, &c., cartage and freight, . . . . . . . . . . .   850 00

| | |
|---|---:|
| Sashes, doors and blinds, ........................ | 368 00 |
| Lathing and plastering, cistern and chimneys, .... | 375 00 |
| Carpenter work, about 275 days, at $3, ........... | 825 00 |
| Painting, ........................................ | 250 00 |
| Plumbing, (pump, sink and piping),.............. | 80 00 |
| Furnace and setting, ............................ | 250 00 |
| Hardware, about, . ............................... | 200 00 |
| Lightning conductors, .......................... | 68 00 |
| Speaking tubes, ................................. | 15 00 |
| The wells walks, grading and gates,.............. | 700 00 |

[*See Details.*]

6*

## 𝔖𝔠𝔞𝔩𝔢 𝔇𝔢𝔱𝔞𝔦𝔩𝔰 𝔣𝔬𝔯 𝔇𝔢𝔰𝔦𝔤𝔫 𝔒𝔫𝔢.

*Fig.* 4.

Fig. 4.—Section, plan and elevation of oriel windows.   Scale, $\frac{1}{8}$ of an inch for one foot.

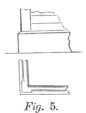

*Fig.* 5.

Fig. 5.—Sill section of lobby entrance. Scale, $\frac{1}{8}$ of an inch for one foot.

*Fig.* 6.

Fig. 6.—Eave and balustrade section of lobby entrance.   Scale, $\frac{3}{16}$ of an inch for one foot.

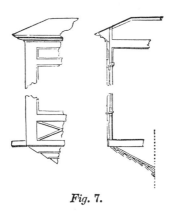

*Fig.* 7.

Fig. 7.—Cross and face section of bay window.   Scale, $\frac{1}{8}$ of an inch for one foot.

*Fig.* 8.

Fig. 8.—Face section of piazza. Scale, ⅛ of an inch for one foot.

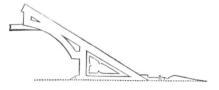

*Fig.* 9.

Fig. 9.—Elevation of gablet verge board and finial. Scale, ⅛ of an inch for one foot.

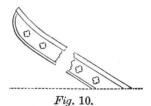

*Fig.* 10.

Fig. 10.—Face section of verge board for the "bell cast" gables, or roof. Scale, ⅛ of an inch for one foot.

*Fig.* 11.

Fig. 11.—Elevation of a window and diagonal paneling underneath the sill. Scale, ⅛ of an inch for one foot.

*Fig.* 1.

## 𝔇esign 𝔗wo.

### A HALF TIMBERED COTTAGE.

————◆————

THE complexion and symmetry of the present design was borrowed from one furnished by the author for a lodge or gatehouse for D. D. Chamberlain, Croton Falls, N. Y., in 1862, and copied in THE WORKING FARMER of that year from the *Horticulturist.* It cost, at Croton Falls, without filling in, $1300. It was built four years ago at Boiling Spring, N. J., and cost, with the present enlargements, about $2000.

Fig. 1.—Is a perspective view of the cottage. 1½ stories high, showing a front dormer which was not in the original design. The foundations are of stone, with a cellar built under the extension. The first story is 9 feet high, the second story is 9 feet in the middle, and 4 feet at the sides of the rooms.

The frame is formed of 2 x 4 "wall strips," and trimmed with *timber casings.*

The lower part weather boarded, horizontally, and the upper part, from the plates, boarded vertically, and furred off from the wall four inches, terminating with a moulding and facia. The roofs project boldly at an angle of 45 degrees, (20 and 24 inches) over the walls, and are covered with pine shingles.

Its cost now would be from $3000 to $3500.

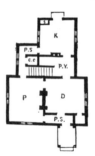

*Fig. 2—First Floor.*

Fig. 2.—P, S, passage from the porch, 4 feet wide; P, parlor, 12x15 feet; D, dining-room, 11½x13 feet, with a china closet, 3x3 feet; P, S, rear passage to kitchen, 4 feet wide, communicating with the stairs to the second floor, and c, c, a coat closet, 3x3 feet; K, kitchen, 12x12 feet; P, Y, pantry, 6x12 feet; S, kitchen-sink and pump.

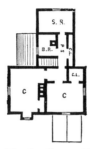

*Fig.* 3—*Second Floor.*

Fig. 3.—P, S, passage, 3 and 5 feet wide, communicating with the bedroom C, 10 x 12 ft., over parlor ; B, R, bath-room, 6 x 6 feet ; S, R, servants' room, 8 x 12 feet ; C, L, are closets.

*( See Details.)*

## Scale Details for Design Two.

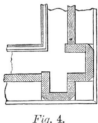

*Fig. 4.*

Fig. 4.—A cross section showing arrangements of timber casings at the corners of the building. Scale, $\frac{3}{4}$ of an inch for one foot.

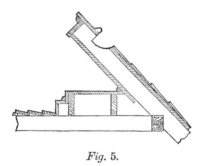

*Fig. 5.*

Fig. 5.—Eave and wall section. Scale, $\frac{1}{2}$ of an inch for one foot.

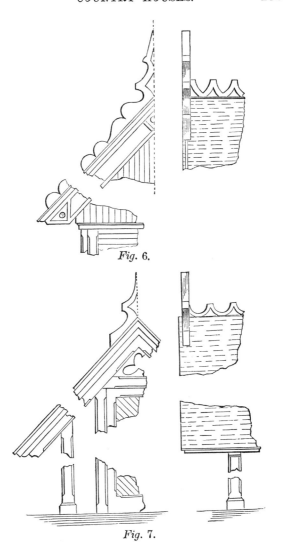

Fig. 6.

Fig. 7.

Fig. 6.—Face and side section, of gable verge board, finial, and pediment. Scale. ¼ of an inch for one foot.

Fig. 7.—Face and side section of entrance porch and door. Scale, ¼ of an inch for one foot.

*Fig.* 8.

Fig. 8.—Cross section, and elevation of window and hood. Scale, ¼ of an inch for one foot.

## Design Three.

## A WORKINGMAN'S COTTAGE.

———∘o⟨∘⟩oo——

WE wish we could plead half as earn-
estly as we feel for a better exhibi-
tion of taste in the cottages of the
working class, for the tenant on the
farm, the estate, and in the town especially.
The popular notion that this class of dwellings
will do of any form, or description of materials, conveys to us the too familiar picture of
a scantling frame packing case, set on a loose
underpinning, and on low ground, boarded
around and covered with a poor shingle roof,
projecting scarcely enough to let the rain drops
clear the wall; barren and disproportioned, a
good house for propagating coarseness within,
and poverty without.

We cannot ascribe the poverty and mean-
ness of most we see, and the scores the trav-

*Fig.* 1.

eling public may see in the towns and villages bordering our railways, to anything but the indifference and selfishness of landlords.

If there is power in fitting forms and color to interest, subdue and educate, why should the home of the laborer and mechanic be made so universally destitute of simple beauty, and as barren as a verdureless field.

If there are such intimate relations between esthetic beauty and moral excellence, why not employ more tact and talent in marrying the useful and beautiful together here?

" *The Workingman's Cottage deserves some serious consideration!*" was the emphatic declaration of one of the most subtile critics of rural art and taste we ever had. It is not necessary to get them up in villa or mansion dress, but relieve their baldness by the introduction of a few simple details, well proportioned, and fittingly applied. In our plan and elevation, we have attempted to show what a cottage of this class may be with reference to outside looks and internal conveniences.

Fig. 1.—Elevation, 1½ stories high, showing

a porch and bay.   First floor, 8 ft. 6 in.; second
floor, 8 ft., in the middle, and 5 at the sides.

*Fig.* 2.

Fig. 2, First floor plan.   P, parlor and dining room, 12 x 12 feet; K, kitchen, 12 x 12
feet; B, R, bed room, 7 x 10 feet; P, pantry,
3 x 8 feet; H, hall, 6 x 7 feet.   A cellar is provided under the whole of the first floor, 6 ft.
6 in. deep, lighted and ventilated.   Second floor
contains three bed rooms and two closets.
Cost $1,400 without filling in, or back plaster.

## 𝔇esign 𝔉our.

### A SEMI-SWISS ORNEE DWELLING.

———•○°○°○○•———

FIGURE 1, is a perspective view, and Fig. 2, 3, and 4 are plans of a "Swiss Orneè" Frame Dwelling, built for the Rev. F. F. Ellinwood, at Orange, N. J. Its location is near the Valley Station of the Morris & Essex R. R., on a fine westerly slope opposite the Orange mountain range, and in the immediate vicinity of extensive suburban improvements projected and carried on by the energy and enterprise of a resident of Orange, J. S. Otis.

The external details of the dwelling, though not clearly indicated in the view, are quite ornate in character, and as a whole add largely to the embellishments and improvements of the neighborhood.

7

Fig. 1.

The dwelling contains fourteen rooms, and cost about $8,500.

The main building is 17 x 36 feet with a dormer lean-to, 9 feet 6 inches wide, which covers the study and a part of the hall. The extension on the opposite side is 16 x 18 feet. The tower, which is a prominent and useful feature, is 12 x 12 and 44 feet high, and located to cover a portion of the hall and command an extensive view of the Orange mountain, "Llewellyn Park," and portions of the upper and lower valley. The stories are respectively 10, 9, and 8 feet. The stories of the tower are 9 feet high each, above the first, which is 10 feet.

The roofs are covered with plain blue and pattern slate, underlaid with tarred paper. The walls are filled in with brick on edge, sided, ceiled, and paneled outside, and lathed and plastered with three-coat work inside, and the entire construction designed to be in all respects workmanlike, substantial and in harmony with the general style.

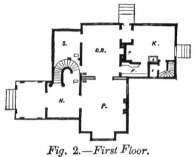

*Fig. 2.—First Floor.*

REFERENCES.

H,  Hall, 11 x 19 feet.

P,  Parlor, 16 x 17 feet.

D, R,  Dining Room, 13 x 16 feet.

K,  Kitchen, 12 x 14 feet.

P,  Pantry, 5 x 9 feet.

C,  Store Closet, $3\frac{1}{2}$ x 5 feet.

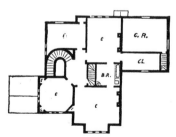

*Fig. 3.—Second Floor.*

C, C, C, C, Sleeping Rooms, 13 x 15, 11 x 11, 9 x 13, and 12 x 14 feet respectively.

B, R, Bath Room, 8 x 9 feet.

C, R, Children's Room, 12 x 15 feet.

C, L, Large Closet, 5½ x 12 feet.

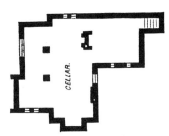

*Fig. 4.—Cellar Plan.*

### ATTIC.

The attic contains three rooms, about 10 x 12 feet, and a tower-loft, 10 x 10 feet.

## Design Five.

## CLEMATIS COTTAGE.

———◦◦⦂●⦂◦◦———

IGURE 1, is a view of a Cottage re-modelled for Jacob Hays, Esq., at In-wood, N. Y., on the Hudson. The main portion, presenting the gable to the front, was built new from the foundations, and the entire cost, in '64, the time at which the remodelling was done, did not exceed $2,800. Naturally, the dwelling at its base, is shut in on the flank, by trees and shrubs, and has a high background of rugged hills; and is not so evenly graded about the front as represented in the view.

Fig. 2, first floor. Rooms as follows: D, R, Dining Room, 15 x 18 feet; S, R, Sewing Room, 10 x 15 feet, with closet; P, P, double Parlor; 15 x 20 feet, with closet. The front lobby, which opens into either room, up stairs and on

*Fig.* **1.**

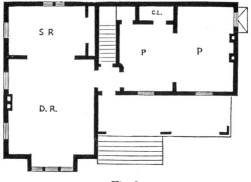

*Fig.* 2.

the porch, is 5 x 6 ft., and tessellated. The back
entry communicates with the passage and
stairs, to the kitchen and cellar in the basement.

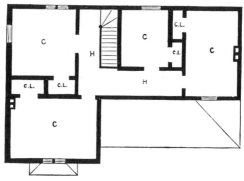

*Fig.* 3.

Fig. 3, chamber floor. C, C, two gable end chambers, 11 x 15 feet, with closets; C, C, two back chambers, 11 x 12 and 10 x 10 feet, with closets; H, hall and passage, 4 feet wide. This hall communicates with two rooms in the attic for servants.

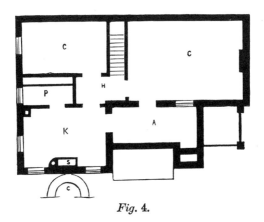

*Fig. 4.*

Fig. 4, basement. K, kitchen, 11 x 14 feet, with pump and sink; P, large pantry; C, C, cellars; A, area, underneath the piazza floor, where there is a water closet.

7*

## Design Six.

## A SYMMETRICAL COTTAGE.

———oo°o°o°oo———

FIGURE 1, is a perspective view of a small symmetrical cottage, designed for a gate-lodge, but adapted to almost any situation in the country ; would do well for a farm, or village tenant, or make a comfortable and tasteful home for the clerk or mechanic just starting in life, and at a cost of about $2,000.

The size of the building is 16 x 26 feet, two stories. First story, 9 feet, second story, 8 feet high, with a cellar 6 feet high, under the whole. The side wings which break the uniformity of outline, giving it a symmetrical cast, are 8, 6 x 13 feet. The piazza is 6½ feet wide, with a simple open timber roof, and in *lieu* of square posts could have rustic ones of cedar or hemlock from the woods.

*Fig.* 1.

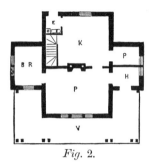

*Fig.* 2.

Fig. 2, is the first floor.    P, parlor, 12 x 15 feet; K, kitchen, 12 x 15 feet; B, R, bed room, 8 x 12 feet; H, lobby or entry, 6 x 8 feet; P, pantry, 6 x 8 feet.

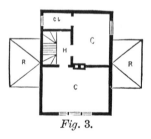

*Fig.* 3.

Fig. 3, second floor, has two bedrooms, one 12 x 15 feet, and one 9 x 12 feet; C, L, closet, 4 x 6 feet; H, hall, 6 feet wide.   The above estimate includes a sink and pump in rear entry, with a 6 x 6 foot cistern, and connections.

## Design Seven.

## A SMALL VILLA OF BROWN STONE.

———o○:̣○○——---

ESIGN 7, is the first of a series made for J. S. Otis, of Orange, N. J., in accordance with a plan for the improvement of his property. It was designed for a family residence, and to be built of Jersey brown stone, which is abundant in the mountain ledges of Orange.

Fig. 1, is a perspective view of the dwelling in the Semi-Gothic style, representing a frontage of 80 feet, and a depth of 30 feet. The stories are, first, 10 feet 6 inches; second, 9 feet 6 inches; attic, 9 feet in the middle. Basement, 8 feet 6 inches high.

Fig. 2. H, hall, 10 feet wide; P, parlor, 14 x 20 feet; D, dining room, 14 x 20 feet; K, kitchen,

*Fig.* 1.

*Fig. 2.—First Floor.*

15x15 feet; C, L, closets; P, Y, large pantry; C, conservatory from dining room.

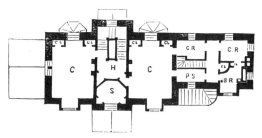

*Fig. 3.—Second Floor.*

Fig. 3.–H, hall, 10 feet wide; S, owner's study, 10 x 10 feet; C, C, principal chambers, 14 x 20feet; C, R, children's rooms, 8 x 10 feet; B, R, bath room, 10 x 12 feet; C, L, closets.

Attic contains three fine rooms; basement contains laundry, second kitchen, and cellar.

## 𝔖𝔠𝔞𝔩𝔢 𝔇𝔢𝔱𝔞𝔦𝔩𝔰 𝔣𝔬𝔯 𝔇𝔢𝔰𝔦𝔤𝔫 𝔖𝔢𝔳𝔢𝔫.

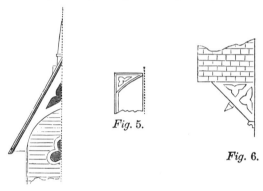

*Fig.* 5.

*Fig.* 6.

*Fig.* 4.

Fig. 4.—Face section of oriel window. Scale, $\frac{1}{8}$ of an inch for one foot.

*Fig.* 7.

*Fig.* 8.

Fig. 5.—Spandrel panels for window heads. Scale, ⅛ of an inch for one foot.

Fig. 6.—Hood bracket. Scale, ⅛ of an inch for one foot.

Fig. 7.—Elevation of front door. Scale, ⅛ of an inch for one foot.

Fig. 8.—Half elevation of pavillion. Scale, ⅛ of an inch for one foot.

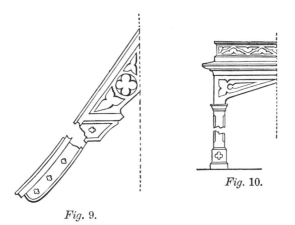

*Fig.* 9.

*Fig.* 10.

Fig. 9.—Face section of verge board. Scale, ⅛ of an inch for one foot.

Fig. 10.—Half elevation of front porch. Scale, ⅛ of an inch for one foot.

## Design Eight.

### A SEASIDE COTTAGE.

BAYSIDE, S. I.

————oo°o°oo————

ROBABLY no section of our country of-
fers such scope for the ingenuity of the
designer in harmonizing architectural
forms with location and scenery, as our
metropolitan suburbs.

Go in any direction we choose within a ra-
dius of 20 or 30 miles from New York, and
we may find sufficient variety in the landscape
to inspire fresh thoughts in the illustration of a
design for a suburban dwelling, and yet architects do not always improve their opportuni-
ties in this respect—either because they have
not visited the site proposed for the dwelling,
—have had no proper description of where it is
to be built, or do not realize that it may ac-

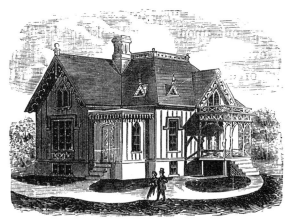

Fig. 1.

quire a character for fitness and harmony by a proper study of the locality.

The annexed design for a seaside cottage, of which Fig. 1 is a perspective view, was built for C. E. Robins, Esq., at Eltingville, Staten Island. It is situated about one thousand feet from the shore of the lower Bay of New York, looking out upon Sandy Hook, the highlands of Nevesink, and the ocean beyond, and in full view of every vessel that enters or leaves the harbor.

The grounds (some nine acres) are tastefully laid out, and the large amount of fruit and ornamental planting—the former of the finest varieties, arranged in quincunx, each row in the order of ripening—and the latter judiciously chosen and effectively disposed in groups and masses—when a few years older, will be very effective as well as valuable.

Fig. 2, represents the first floor, enclosing an area which includes the extent of the building in compact form, 25 feet front, by 35 feet deep. L, lobby, 6 x 6 feet; P, parlor, 15 x 15 feet; D, R, dining room, 15 x 19 feet, with

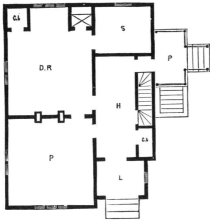

*Fig. 2.*

closet, 3½ feet, and a waiter; S, study, 8 x 9 feet; H, hall, 8 x 17 feet; P, porch, 6 x 10 feet.

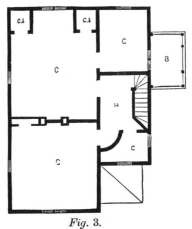

*Fig. 3.*

Fig. 3, second floor. H, hall; C, C, C, bed-rooms, 15 x 15, 15 x 19, and 8 x 10 feet respectively; B, balcony, 6 x 10 feet, railed; C, L, closets, 3½ feet each.

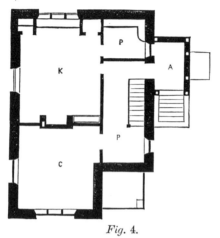

*Fig.* 4.

Fig. 4, basement. A, area, 5 x 8 feet; P, passage or hall, 7 x 17 feet, communicating with cellar and milk-room in the front; K, kitchen, 14 x 18 feet; P, pantry, 7 x 7½ feet; C, cellar, 13 x 13 feet.*    The dwelling is 25 x 35 feet; 1½ stories high; 1st story 9 feet; 2d story, 8½ feet at the plates. The follow-

* Some changes were made, including more closet room, than the engraved plan shows

ing gives a condensed view of the desirable points of the dwelling:

1. Two balconies, looking out on the ocean.

2. The building stands so related to the points of the compass that the sun shines on every side during a part of every 24 hours.

3. Fourteen closets, most of them of large capacity.

4. Rain and slop cisterns, sink and water in kitchen.

5. Study, or library, is fitted up to be used as an office or business room, bracketed shelves for law and business books, and miscellaneous library with glass doors, letter press and large writing desk, also clothes-closet behind waiter, answering to a vault for books and papers of account, etc.

6. Attic, under deck or flat, finished as ser-vants' sleeping room.

7. Shelved milk-room.

8. But one chimney stack.

9. Filled in with hard brick.

10. House and adjacent ground thoroughly drained with stone and tile drains.

The entire cost, as above described, foots up within $4,500.

We give the following letter from Mr. Robins, who has kindly permitted us to publish it:

N. Y., *Nov.* 4, 1867.

D. T. ATWOOD, Esq.:

Dear Sir:—The lodge and stable recently completed for me at Bay Side, have elicited general and marked commendation from those whose opinion is more valuable, as being less likely to be partial, than mine. Our friends generally express surprise at the capacity and convenient arrangement of the rooms in the lodge, and particularly at the size. Among many other excellencies, I think that this is the peculiar merit of both these buildings—and it is just the point in which there are the greatest number of architectural failures. It is an easy matter for any draughtsman to get up a showy facade; but to combine harmoniously beauty with *use*, to make a comparatively inexpensive dwelling, symmetrical and graceful in its outlines, and thoroughly comfortable to live in, requires some study, and in a small house, more professional ability than in a large one. I will add, after two months occupancy, which is the architect's highest praise, that I see nothing to improve in the form or arrangement of either building, and had I to erect them again, I would simply duplicate your plans. Very truly,

C. E. ROBINS.

The following is the elevation of the stable erected at the same time.

## Design Nine.

## A SUBURBAN STABLE.

————o-o⚬⚬o-o————

WE may remark, that buildings in the suburbs of our large cities are no longer the distasteful objects they were half a generation ago, or before business and professional men sought in earnest the recuperative enjoyments of suburban and country life.

Outbuildings particularly were inconvenient and expressionless. Now they are as definitively classed as any in the architectural series, and in order that they may harmonize with the modern dwelling, it becomes the duty of the designer to clothe them with some permanent marks of beauty, culture, refinement, home-comfort, fitness.

8

*Fig.* 1.

This design gives evidence of a more careful study than such buildings commonly receive. It was originally to have been built of concrete, with hard burned brick facings, window and door jambs, and quoins; but on account of the difficulty experienced in obtaining the labor sufficiently skilled in that class of work, it was executed in wood with vertically boarded and battened walls, and slate roofs. Cost, $2,200.

Fig. 1, is the elevation of the entrance front towards the Lodge and Dwelling. The building is 30 x 30 feet, and 16 feet high from the water-table to the plates. The roof is fixed at a quarter pitch, and projected boldly at the eaves, and is surmounted with a concave roof ventilator, 12 x 12 feet, and upon this a wren turret. Referring to the plans,

Fig. 2, is the first floor, with coach room, tool room, six stalls, and stairs to the basement.

Fig. 3, is the second floor, with man's room, feed-bins, and a spacious loft properly lighted and thoroughly ventilated. The water which falls upon the roof is conducted to a large cistern provided with a chain pump.

In the barnyar l is the pig-pen, corn-crib, and manure cistern, with every convenience for facilitating and saving labor about the stable.

*Fig. 2.— First Floor.*

REFERENCES.

1,  Coach Room, $14\frac{1}{2}$ x 20 feet.

2,  Tool Room, 8 x 9 feet.

3,  Stalls, $4\frac{1}{2}$ and 5 x 8 feet, and passage 5 x 29 feet.

*Fig. 3.— Second Floor.*

1,  Man's room, 8 x 9 feet.

2,  Loft, 20 x 29 feet, 6 feet at the plates, and 15 feet high under the ventilator.

3,  Feed Bin.

## 𝔖𝔠𝔞𝔩𝔢 𝔇𝔢𝔱𝔞𝔦𝔩𝔰 𝔣𝔬𝔯 𝔇𝔢𝔰𝔦𝔤𝔫 𝔑𝔦𝔫𝔢.

*Fig* 4.

Fig. 4.—Elevation of one half the ventilator. Scale, ⅛ of an inch for one foot.

*Fig.* 5.

Fig. 5.—Eave section, showing projection, &c., of cornice. Scale, ⅛ of an inch for one foot.

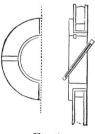

*Fig.* 6.

Fig. 6.—Vertical section and half face view of loft windows.   Scale, ¼ of an inch for one foot.

## Design Ten.

## A COUNTRY CHURCH.

———∘o⦂⊙⦂oo——

E offer the accompanying design of a Country Chapel, with lecture-room attached, as a fair type of what such structures should be.  It at least fills our conception of the harmonious in country life and worship.

We would not have for this purpose, in any rural district, a stately or costly edifice to nourish the pride of a few and discourage the many.  Humility and simplicity should be the ruling thought in all our rural chapels, in the arrangement of their proportions, and in their decorations.  We would not deny enough of ecclesiastical dignity to indicate the purpose of the building, because this would be admissi-

*Fig.* 1.

ble and consistent. But we would try to em-
body that sentiment of the human heart which
endorses the equality of all loving souls towards
the Master, so that if the building could utter
any language it would be a hearty and emphatic invitation to enter and praise the Great
Author of our being.

We love low eave-lines, as speaking to us
of the hand which reaches low to lift the hum-
blest; and the high roof, indicative of that full
and compassionate protection whose unvarying
lines meet at the summit of perfection—Truth
—and the trim spire reaching modestly above
the rooftrees of the village dwellings, rendering
unnecessary the oft repeated question, "Where
is your Church."

The design, of which Fig. 1 is a perspective
view, was the first prepared for the Carmel M.
E. Church, Putnam Co., N. Y., but being
deemed inadequate to the wants of a large and
populous parish, was superseded by a larger
one, on the same ground plan, and executed in
stone, quarried from the neighborhood.

Fig. 2.—The plan, is $40 \times 70$ feet, for audito-

8*

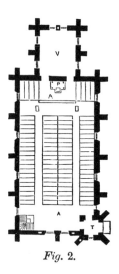

*Fig.* 2.

rium and 16 x 24 feet for lecture and school-
room. The audience room will seat 350 to
400 persons. There are no galleries, only an
organ and choir loft over the lobby. The interior is finished in chestnut, oiled; the roof
open, and ceiled from wall plates to ridge pole.
The cost of this chapel in any convenient suburban district, two to four hours from New
York, would be about $15,000.

## 𝔇𝔢𝔰𝔦𝔤𝔫 𝔈𝔩𝔢𝔳𝔢𝔫.

## A COUNTRY CHURCH.

————∘∘⦂⬥⦂∘∘————

REW M. E. CHURCH. Thus stands the title on the mural tablet over the doorway of a church edifice of pleasing proportions and excellent construction in the beautiful village of Carmel, Putnam Co., New York—built mainly by the munificent contributions of its founder, Daniel Drew, Esq., for the Methodist Episcopal Parish of that place.

It is chiefly interesting to the architect and connoisseur, as an example of how the earliest pointed Gothic architecture, devoid of decoration, may be economically adapted to the needs of an American Parish—serve the interests of congregational worship of to-day, and

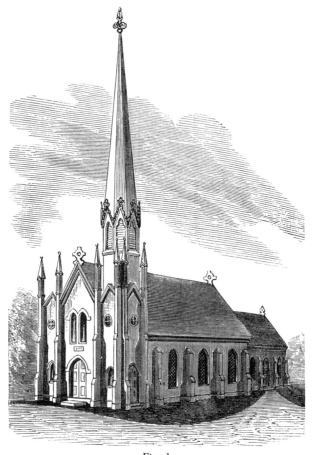

*Fig.* 1.

at the same time preserve the essential part of that sentiment of structural worship, and aspiring praise, developed through the progress of church art, from the opening portal of the first Christian church, to the consummated idea of temple worship, realized in those grandly overarching vaultings of the Gothic nave.

In this example the form has been harmonized to meet what was considered desirable acoustic properties, and the wants of that individual parish.

The proportions of the Church are, for the length, a little over a cube and one half, or 70 feet; and the height about a cube, or 44 feet, from the auditorium to the centre of the arched ceiling. The width is also 44 feet, giving an oblong plan; a vestry room at the rear, 30 x 40 feet; and a clear and spacious audience room, unobstructed by columns, and spaned by a tudor-arched ceiling, supported at intervals of 12 feet, by heavy timbered principal rafters exposed below the ceiling, stained and varnished.

The interior of the church is finished plainly

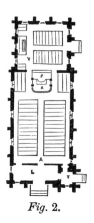

*Fig.* 2.

yet handsomely, and in keeping with the simplicity of the exterior.

The pulpit and altar are finished with black
walnut, with a frescoed reredos at the back.

Over the lobby opposite is the organ loft,
communicated with from below. The ceilings
are richly frescoed in panels between the prin-
cipals, on a light blue ground, and the side
walls colored a light warm drab in distemper.
Windows are filled in with stained glass, and
the trefoil and quarter-foil apertures with flam-
boyant patterns, by Hamilton & Son. Pews
are of pine, with black walnut trimmings,
oiled and varnished. Aisles are paved with

Minton's encaustic tiles. For heating and ventilating ample provisions have been made, and the building thus affords the means of worship to a congregation of from 500 to 700 persons, at a cost not exceeding $40,000, including the iron fencing and gates for both church and parsonage.

Externally, the prominent feature is the tower and spire, on the right front corner, 100 feet high, forming one of the side entrances to the lobby, and a conspicuous mark for miles around, and in pleasing contrast with the strangely picturesque scenery of the hills.

An attempt to symmetrize the front will be observed on the left of the middle entrance, by carrying up a buttressed wall vail, a practice not uncommon, but questionable in an esthetic sense, in so small a building. The walls of the building were built entirely of stone, in random course, with hammered stone dressings, taken from the immense beds of drift rock and granitic nuclei existing in the neighborhood.

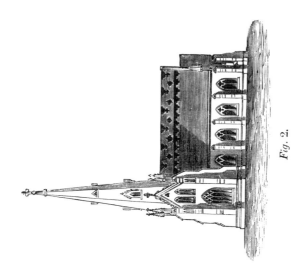

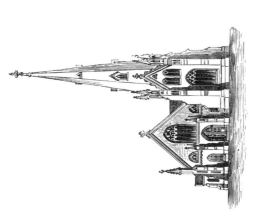

Fig. 1.

Fig. 2.

## 𝔇esign 𝔗welve.

## A COUNTRY CHURCH.

---

### REFERENCES.

FIGURE 1, front elevation of the Presbyterian Parish Church, at Goshen, Orange Co., N. Y.

Fig. 2, side elevation of the same.

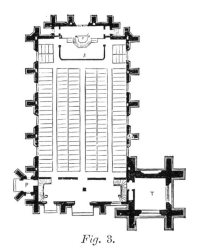

*Fig. 3.*

Fig. 3.—Plan.

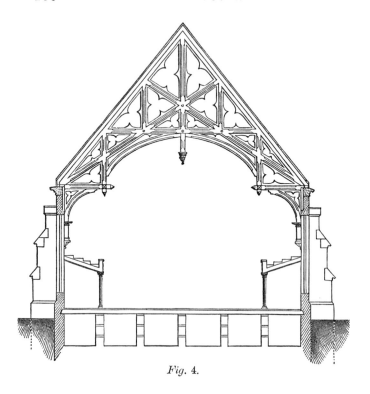

*Fig.* 4.

Fig. 4.—Transverse section, showing open timber roof, walls and buttresses. Scale 24 feet to one inch.

# Specifications

## FOR THE GOSHEN PRESBYTERIAN CHURCH.

### DIMENSIONS.

Outside size of Church, 66 x 109 feet. Outside of tower, 30 x 30 feet. Height of side walls, 33 feet, and height of gable ends from the ground level to apex, 70 feet.

Height of the tower and spire inclusive, 180 feet, or six times its diameter from the ground line to the apex, or finial.

The audience room will be 62 x 90 feet, and covered with an open timbered roof. Lobby 15 x 62 feet.

There will be an altar recess, as per plan, with an altar window. Also, an organ loft and side galleries.

### CHAPEL PLANS.

Plans for a chapel accompanying the church plans, providing for a lecture room on first floor, 36 x 50, and a school room on 2d floor, 36 x 58 feet. All in the pointed Gothic Style of Architecture. The Church plans are drawn to a scale for ground plan of $\frac{1}{8}$ of an inch for 1 foot, and for elevations 3-32 of an inch for 1 foot. The Chapel plans are all drawn to a scale of 3-32 of an inch for 1 foot, or 16 feet to $1\frac{1}{2}$ inches of the rule, or scale. [See Plans.]

### MASON WORK.

Excavate for a basement under the audience room 8 feet deep below the audience floor. Excavate for 4 x 4 feet areas on each side, to light the same; also, for entrance area on left side, or side opposite the tower, 6 x 10 feet. Excavate for the tower and foundations, as per plans, allowing 18 inches on all sides for footings. Excavate for the tower foundations to a depth of 8 feet, and for all other foundations, including those of the chapel, to a depth of 5 feet below the grade; make all required excavations for drains, flues, piers, required to make the work complete. Excavate for a cistern 10 feet in diameter, and 10 feet deep; also, for a cess-pool 6 x 8 feet, at the rear of building, as directed.

### STONE WORK

Will be according to plans and working drawings, and of the blue stone quarried in the neighborhood of Goshen, N. Y. The body of all the walls and backing up will be of rubble stone as it comes from the quarry. All the base and string courses, arch stones, archivolts, buttress-caps, sills and quoin stones, will be dressed or tooled, worked plain and rough to beds and joints. Pinacles and finials will be wrought of stone, and the spire will be built of stone worked plain and rough to beds and joints, all in accordance with the working drawings.

### FOOTINGS.

Build all the footings of rubble stone, laid up in cement mortar, and broad enough to project six inches on each side of all foundations of the body walls or buttresses, and 30 inches deep, or high, for all except tower foundations, these to have footings 4 feet high. For the basement walls the footings must be placed below the depth specified for the excavation.

### THICKNESS OF WALLS.

Build the walls for the body of church and chapel 24 inches thick above the base, and from thence to the plates and ridges, except on the front, where archivolts are formed around the entrances, and capped with string courses. Walls around middle front entrance to be 4 feet thick, and around side walls 3 feet thick, as per elevation.

### BASE COURSE.

Project the base course, also the foundations all around, 6 inches outside the superstructure walls, as shown. The sub-base for tower, has a moulded member which will project 3 inches beyond the superstructure, making altogether a 9 inch projection around the superstructure of the tower, as shown. Build the walls of the tower above the foundations and base 4 feet thick, and draw in at the four corners at the junction of the spire to receive the same in the form of an octagon, as shown. Build the body of the tower 64 feet high from the grade to spire base, and carry up the gable or pediment walls on all sides, so as to make their height from the grade 77 feet. Build the spire of stone, leaving dormer openings, as per elevations, and 110 feet from the top of the buttresses to the finial. Build the base of spire walls at the starting 4 feet thick on every side, and diminish uniformly to 3 feet at the top. Lay all the stone in the best cement mortar, and bind as directed by the details. Work a finial of stone, and secure the same by a long anchor-rod of wrought iron, passing through the point down inside and secured with a sufficient weight, as directed. Diameter of the finial stem will be 20 to 24 inches. See working sections of spire and spire base.

### BUTTRESSES.

Build buttresses for the main building 3 x 6 feet. For the chapel 2½ x 5 feet. For the tower 4 x 8, with "set-off," face as shown, and capped with worked blue stone caps as per detail.

### STONE CORNICES AND FINIALS.

Provide and fix stone eave and raking cornices 12 x 20 inches, and of stone broad enough on the gables to form a coping 30 inches wide. Surmount the front apex with a stone *cruciform* finial, as shown, 12 inches thick. Surmount the angle buttresses with octagonal turret points 4 feet in diameter at the base. Build octagonal turrets 8 feet in diameter at the front angles of the chapel, of stone, one surmounted with a spire point, and the other capped with a flat octagonal cap of cut stone, as shown. [See details.]

### OPENINGS.

Leave openings in the walls, as per plan, for doors and windows. Side window openings for audience room will be 8 x 20 feet. For the chapel, 6 x 20 feet. For the tower-room, 12 x 26 feet. For the organ loft, 14 x 26 feet. For the altar recess, 15 x 30 feet. The opening for the middle entrance doors is 10 x 20 feet, and the opening for side doors, 6 x 15 feet.

### POINTING WITH CEMENT.

Point up all stone work, after the walls are completed (except spires), with cement mortar, colored, to produce a gray joint; clean out and wash the lime joints before pointing.

### IRON WORK.

Provide and fix all necessary iron anchors, stirrups, camps, &c., required by working plans to bind the stone work together. Have the carpenter, or notify him, to place wooden bonds as the work progresses, etc.

### BRICK WORK.

Provide and lay the lobby partition wall, supporting organ loft, of hard brick, starting on a stone wall 18 inches thick in the basement; build said wall 12 inches thick, leaving door openings, as per plan. Lay an 8 inch brick backing to form the box for sliding entrance doors, as shown. Lay brick piers for the support of the audience room floor 20 x 20 inches, and 24 x 24. Form the smoke flues of hard brick. Lay all inside skew back, lintel or other constructive arches, of hard brick.

### CISTERN.

Build the cistern of brick, laying an 8 inch side wall and covering with a segmental arch of brick in the usual manner. Plaster to make water tight, and provide and lay the necessary supply and waste drains.

### CESS-POOL.

Build the cess-pool, if one is required, of rough stone, and cover with broad flat stone.

### FLUES, &c.

Form a niche and closet in the tower wall, as per plan, and build ventilating flues, as per plans, for the admission of fresh air, and to conduct the foul air from the rooms.

### STEPS.

Build, or provide and fix plain cut stone steps for all door openings as per plans, the last step to form a platform of the size on the plan.

Lath and plaster side walls (on furring) in the audience. lecture and school rooms, tower room, and on the ceilings between the principal rafters and frame work, with the best three-coat work, consisting of a coat of scratch, a brown coat, well floated and straightened, to receive the last coat which will be the hard finish. The angles and corners of all window jambs will be trimmed with a Gothic ret bead, and the plaster "flushed up" to them.

### DEAFEN.

Deafen the floors of the audience room, chapel, galleries and tower, over proper "sound boarding," to be put in by the carpenter. Use "coarse stuff;" and lay a thickness of 3 inches between each beam.

### GROUT, &c.

Grout the cellar bottom or basement, also the areas, and plaster the side and end walls. Lath and plaster the ceiling of the basement.

### AREAS.

Build the areas for windows and doors, as per plan, and cap with large flat blue stone 4 to 6 inches thick. Provide and fix coal-shoots, and cold air box openings, as per basement plan.

### CARPENTER WORK—TIMBER AND FRAMING.

Provide spruce timber and scantlings for floors, partitions and girders and for the lighter portion of the roof; provide pine for the balance. Floor beams must be 3 x 12 inches, placed 12 inches apart from centers, bridged every 10 feet; and the audience floor supported by three tiers of girders 6 x 10 inches, resting on brick piers in the basement, 8 feet apart. Scantling for gallery floors must be 4 x 6 inches, and 4 x 8 inches, and furring off do, 2 x 4 and 3 x 4 inches. Plates 4 x 12 to lay on the wall and anchor thereto. For the roof of church and chapel, provide the following sizes: Principal rafters over the open timbers 5 x 12 inches, common do. 3 x 6 inches, purlins 4 x 10 inches, ridge-pole 4 x 10 inches. For sizes of open timber roof, see plan of same.

### ROOFING.

Provide and frame open timber principal rafters of pine, as per detail, and indicated by following figure. Plane off all the timbers to receive paint and stains, and fill in with 2 and 3 inch quarter and trefoil panels, with margins chamfered; support each end of the hammer beam with column, as per detail, 8 inches in diameter, resting upon stone corbels projecting from the walls. Secure all joints of the framework with wrought anchors and bands made to accommodate the various angles of the pieces, and bolted through from side to side.

Over the principal rafters place the common do., purlins and jack rafters, the latter lay on purlins 16 inches from centers up and down, and cover the whole roof with common, mill worked pine boards.

Build chapel roof in the same manner and style, as per framing plans, and cover the whole with Pennsylvania blue slate, with bands to relieve in cruciform and triangular patterns, as shown; size of slates, 8 x 16 inches.

Provide and lay tarred paper, or a paper saturated with tar, before laying the slate, properly lapped and secured to the roof boarding. Use galvanized iron nails, not less than 4d size, and not less than 2 nails to each slate. Provide 6℔ lead flashings and valleys, also gutters, as per details.

### FLOORS.

Provide and lay 1¼ x 3 and 4 inch mill-worked, first quality pine flooring for all floors, except lobbys and porch entrance. Bridge all floor beams every 10 feet apart, and blind nail with 10d nails; smooth off the joints at completion.

### TILE.

Provide and lay Minton's tile, No. 2 pattern, in the lobbys of church and chapel, and in porch.

### GALLERIES.

Provide and fix side galleries in the audience room, on each side, 10 feet wide, 9 feet high from the floor on the front, and 12 feet high at the back, or against the wall. Support the same with six Gothic columns of cast iron, three on each side; construct the frame work of 4 x 6 and 8 inch scantlings, with framed trusses from column to column. Divide the width into 4 tiers of pews rising one above the other 9 inches each, or an aggregate rise of 36 inches. Construct the pews to correspond with those of the audience floor. Cut and wainscot the inside, and panel the outside with Gothic trefoil panels, as per details. Build the organ loft or gallery on the same general plan, wide enough to cover the lobby, with the middle space fitted up for the organ and choir, and the ends with pews. Provide 3 x 12 floor beams for the floor, and construct the frame and other work according to the working plan; panel the front to correspond with the side galleries.

### STAIRS.

Build quarter circle stairs, as per plan, (or the ascent may be changed if any other form be thought more convenient)

9

42 inches wide in the usual manner, with a close string and close ceiled and paneled rail, as per details. Rail-cap to be of black walnut, and oiled; the other parts built of clear seasoned pine; the steps to be nosed and coved, and covered with Snow's patent "Brass Stair Facings." Build chapel stairs in the same manner, as per plans. Build a plain flight of basement stairs under the lobby stairs of the church.

### WAINSCOT.

Wainscot the entire church and chapel, 1st and 2d floors with seasoned and clear pine, 3 inches wide to the window stools, and 20 inches high in the school room of chapel opposite each window, and 36 inches elsewhere, trimmed with a cap.

### TRIMMINGS AND ARCHITRAVES.

Trim all the window openings with returned Gothic beads 2 inches in diameter at the juncture of the jamb and face of the wall, the side jambs to be plastered. Trim the bottom of the windows with heavy 2 inch beveled stools coinciding with cap of wainscot. Trim all doors with 6 inch double moulded architraves, as per detail.

### FRAMES.

Build the large and small window frames, as shown by the elevations, of pine plank, with heavily moulded casings and mullions, with 4 to 6 inches face, and jambs 8 to 12 inches deep, with pointed, and trefoil heads to fill the different openings, as per details.

### BELFRY FRAMES.

The double upper tower windows will be filled in with broad slats to keep out the storm and to permit flow of sound outward.

### METAL SASHES.

All windows (except basement) will be filled in with metal and wood sashes, glazed with plain ground and stained glass, diamond or other shape. The altar window will be glazed with a figured stained glass in different designs, as shown in the details. Basement sashes and frames will be of ordinary construction, glazed with extra thick American window glass, hung with weights. Metal sashes will be provided with sections for opening above and below, as per detail.

### DOORS.

Provide and fix outside doors of oak, 2½ and 3 inches thick, panel-moulded with heavy Gothic flush moulds; those of the church lobby to slide in the wall, in the manner of sliding doors, and to be trimmed with heavy locks and plated knobs of the best manufacture, and provided with spring and flush bolts. The middle entrance and side doors of the church to be separated by a joint at the spring of the arch, as shown. All the interior doors to be 2 inches thick, 4 and 12 paneled, of pine, and R. M. hung with strong 5 inch loose joint butts, and trimmed with the best 6 inch mortice locks, and white porcelain furniture. The doors opening from the chapel and church lobbys into the audience and lecture rooms will be folding doors, or double and in pairs; others will be single, all in accordance with details and schedule.

### PEWS.

Build pews of clear pine, * with black walnut cap rails, on the backs and pew ends 2½ x 2 inches, as per details, located on the floors, as per plans, 30 inches from back to back, allowing 15 inches for the seat, and 15 inches for foot space, and 18 to 20 sidewise for each person. Pew ends will be ornamental, and 1½ inches thick, rounded and chamfered, backs 1 inch thick, and seats 1¼ inch; backs and seats inclined at an angle to make sitting most natural and

---

* Oiled Chestnut may be substituted for interior wood finish, if church committee deem advisable, and authorize the additional outlay.

comfortable. All pew backs are to be provided with hard wood book-holders, one half the length of each pew, and each pew with one foot stool, of pine, half the length of pew.

### PULPIT OR DESK, AND ALTAR RAIL.

Provide and lay the altar floor, enclosed with a 6 inch black walnut rail, and 3 inch balusters, 7 inches from the audience floor, as per plan, and the altar recess floor back of the desk 24 inches from said floor, panel the rise on each side with Gothic panel work, and provide steps 6 x 12 inches to the upper floor, as per plan.

### DESK.

Build an octagonal desk or pulpit of black walnut, with paneled base and sides, and richly moulded cap; size, 8 feet in diameter at the base, and 6 feet at the top. Make the top of the desk 30 inches high above the recess floor. Provide newels for the altar rails 12 inches in diameter at the base, and 10 inches through the shaft. Place the balusters 3 inches apart; oil and polish all the black walnut work about the altar and pulpit, as directed. Provide and fit up the recess closets, enlarged 2 feet more than shown by the plan, as directed. The wall of the closets will be but 10 feet high, and the outside screened or cased with Gothic paneled wainscot, extending around the entire recess in imitation of chapel screens, for construction of which see details.

### CHAPEL DESKS.

Provide plain pine moulded and paneled desks, for the lecture and school rooms, set upon a platform 8 inches high from the floor; desks 32 inches high from the platform, and of the size on the plan.

### VENTILATION.

Provide and fix ventilating flues and registers, 12 in number, as directed per details.

### FURNACES.

Provide and set two portable furnaces in the basement, to heat the audience room and lobbies, of sufficient capacity to supply 15 registers, placed in the floor, 12 x 18 inches each.

### SEXTON'S ROOM.

Provide and finish off plainly in the basement, as directed, a sexton's room 12 x 12 feet, sufficiently lighted and ventilated, and supplied with a bell from the pastor's closet.

### BELL.

Provide and fix a tower bell, the best Troy manufacture, with an 8 feet wheel, and to weigh 800 ℔s, properly set, under the supervision of the committee and architect. The necessary girders and floor beams being previously set for its support.

### STEPS.

Provide a flight of steps for the tower loft and bell room, and also to ascend to the highest openings in the spire.— Build plain, and of strong pine plank, 1½ inches thick, as directed; the first flight starting from the organ loft.

### PAINTING.

Paint all outside wood work except hard wood doors, which will be oiled thoroughly, 3 coats of gray, using pure lead and oil. Shellac and stain the interior—except hard wood—two coats, with oil and sienna, after all work has been thoroughly smoothed and cleaned off with sand paper. The open timber roofs will be treated in the same manner, and varnished three coats. All the interior finish not in immediate contact with feet or hands, will receive three coats of varnish, as gallery fronts, doors and architraves and cornice moulds between the principal rafters.

Paint the walls and ceiling two coats of gray, in size, or oil fresco, as shall be hereafter decided. Paint all metal work exposed to the weather, two coats of Prince's Metalic

Paint. Paint the stairs two coats of gray, also basement wood-work, and the close strings and rails may be stained or grained.

### PLUMBING.

Provide a No. 4 Douglas force and lift pump, brass chamber, over an iron sink, 20 x 41½ inches in the sexton's room, supplied from the cistern, by a 1½ inch lead pipe. Provide and fix a bowl and faucet, also a small water tank in the pastor's closet, with waste going to the cess-pool, and supply from the tank over the wash bowl.

### GUTTERS OF LEAD.

Gutters of lead will be formed in such portions of the eaves as will be deemed most practicable to supply said cistern.

### HOSE.

A hose must be provided and attached to the pump, for the purpose of cleaning windows and areas, and to use in case of fire.

NOTE.—Since preparing design 12 for publication, the estimated cost being more than the Building Committee were authorized to expend, they have reconsidered their resolution to build this design and have adopted a second design prepared by the author and now in process of erection. The general plan being the same, it was not thought advisable to re-engrave for the changes, internally or externally.

## Design Thirteen.

## A FARM BARN.

———◦◦❭❀❬◦◦———

THERE are few objects in the country districts that command our sympathies and excite our interest more than the farm buildings erected for grain and stock.

Without pretending to style or architectural beauty, they form harmonious and interesting features in our rural landscape, and appeal strongly to our national taste for breadth, abundance, and thrift.

The accompanying plan is not offered as a model, though a very good one for a grain and stock farm, and designed for one of the grain growing sections of New York State. A glance at the plan will show in the main building the

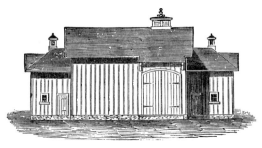

*Fig.* 1

old-fashioned bay and threshing floor, borrowed from our German and English neighbors, and retained by us as an essential feature of the Yankee system of barn building. The main building of our plan is 34 x 44 feet fronting north-east, with wing-extensions on each side 18 x 66 feet, running southwest, in which provision is made for stock, feed, and grain. One side on the southwest forms an L 40 feet long. These extensions are 1½ stories high, with cellars for roots, and manure pits, below the first floor. Posts of extensions are 16 feet high, and posts of main building 24 feet high, giving abundant loft room.

REFERENCES.

Fig. 1, is the front elevation showing vertically boarded and battened walls, shingle roofs, and ventilators. The frame is heavily timbered, taken from the forest and framed in the old style with 12 x 12 sills, 8 x 8 posts, 6 x 6 girths, and purlins 8 x 12, plates 4 x 6, braces.

Fig. 2, is the first or ground floor plan: T, R, threshing room, or floor, 16 x 32 feet; B,

9*

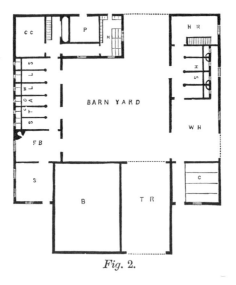

*Fig.* 2.

granary with bins, 13 x 16 feet; W, H, wagon house, 16 x 20 feet; H, S, stalls, 5 feet wide; H, R, harness room, 10 x 16 feet, with stairs to the loft; F, R, feed room, (with boiler), 12 x 16 feet, and a range of cattle stalls adjoining, 4 feet wide each; C, C, corn crib, 10 x 15 feet; P, pig-pen, 12 x 12 feet; H, hennery, 10 x 15 feet. The entire range of buildings are well ventilated and lighted. A large water tank is placed in the barn yard into which the rain water is conducted from the roofs, one half of the tank is arranged as a filter, the other half as a pure water compartment, from which the water to be used is drawn.

The cost of this barn, where the timber could be cut from the farm, and rough lumber procured from the neighboring saw-mills, would be about $2,000.

## Design Fourteen.

### A COUNTRY GENTLEMAN'S STABLE.

———o◦:◦:◦o———

FIGURE 1, is a perspective view of a large double stable, designed for D. D. Chamberlain, Croton Falls, N. Y., and intended to embrace every modern improvement in stable-fitting worth having, combined with the most perfect facilities for ventilating, the care of horses, and the housing of vehicles. Size of building, 74 x 84 feet. First story 15 feet, second story 10 feet. Walls built of hard brick, and hollow.

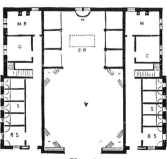

*Fig. 2.*

*Fig.* 1.

Fig. 2,—Plan.   V, vestibule, 40 x 40  feet; lighted from the dome above the roof.   1,1,1, 1, harness closets, with glass sliding doors; C, R, coach room, 30 x 40 feet, with stalls for vehicles, and space for washing the same; W, water in coach room; S, stalls, 6 x 10 feet; right hand range for owner, left hand range for guests; B, S, box stalls, 10 x 10 feet; G, grainery, 13 x 13 feet ; M, R, man's or groom's room, 13 x 18 feet, made fire proof.   Under the loft stairs is placed a water-closet, urinal, wash-basin, and an additional water tank. Root and manure cellars are beneath the first floor.

Cost estimated at $15,000.

*Design Fifteen.   Fig.* **1.**

## Design Fifteen.

### SMALL SUBURBAN STABLE.

———∽∘⦂◦⦂∘∾———

FIGURE 1, is the elevation of a small wooden stable, 18 x 28 feet, and open shed, 12 x 15 feet. One and a half stories high, with ventilator. Designed and built for D. D. Chamberlain, Croton Falls, N. Y. Also for C. E. Parker, Rutherford Park, N. J., at a cost of $550.

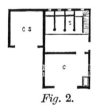

*Fig.* 2.

Fig. 2.—The plan. C, carriage room, 16 x 14 feet; S, stalls, 4½ x 9 feet; C, S, cow shed, 12 x 15 feet. Feed bin is placed under the stairs, and the harness closet in carriage room.

## Design Sixteen.

## SMALL SUBURBAN STABLE.

———◦◦⟡◦◦———

FIGURE 1, elevation of a small suburban stable, 20 x 30 feet, one and a half stories. Hen-house, 12 x 20 feet. Pigpen, 10 x 10 feet.

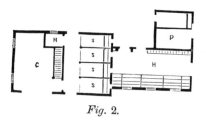

*Fig.* 2.

Fig. 2.—The plan. C, carriage room, 18 x 15 feet; S, stalls, 5 x 9 feet; H, harness closet; H, hen-house; P, piggery. Feed bin in the loft, with shoots to lower the grain.

*Fig.* 1.

## Design Seventeen.

## BOWLING ALLEY.

———o○o○——

IGURE 1, perspective view of a Bowling Alley, 13 x 97 feet, designed for D. D. Chamberlain, Croton Falls, N. Y. Lighted principally from the roof.

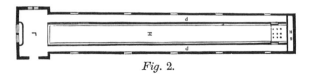

*Fig.* 2.

Fig. 2.—The plan.   L, lobby entrance, 10x15 feet; H, bowling track, 86 feet long and 4 feet wide, between the racks a ball holder; P, P, passages, 3 feet wide on each side of track; B, H, bulk head and bowling pit.

*Fig.* 1.

## Design Eighteen.

## RESIDENCE OF C. E. ROBINS.

———◦◦✿◦◦———

Fig. 1.—Entrance Front Elevation.

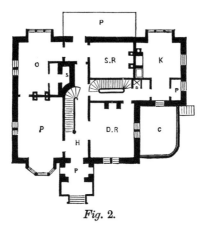

*Fig. 2.*

Fig. 2.—Plan of First Floor.

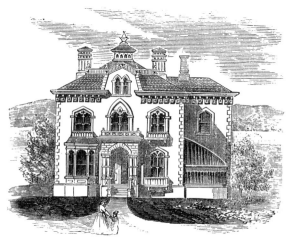

*Fig.* 1.

REFERENCES.

P, porch; H, hall; P, parlor, 15 x 20 feet; D, R, dining room, 15 x 18 feet; O, office, or library, 15 x 17 feet; S, safe, or vault for office; S, R, sitting room, 12 x 15 feet; K, kitchen, 15 x 15 feet; P, pantry, 3 x 6 feet; D, waiter and china closet.

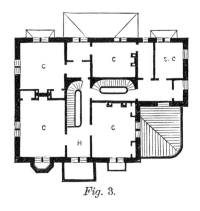

*Fig.* 3.

Fig. 3.—Plan of Second Floor. C, C, C, C, chambers, 12 x 15, 15 x 19, and 15 x 16 feet; S, C, servant's chamber. 10 x 12 feet; H, hall.

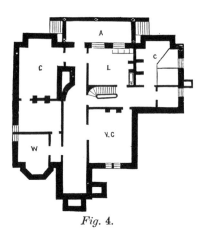

*Fig.* 4.

Fig. 4.—Basement Plan.  W, wine cellar, 10 x 12 feet;  V, C, vegetable cellar, 15 x 18 feet;  L, laundry, 12 x 15 feet; C, C, cellars, 15 x 17 and 15 x 20 feet.

[*See Specifications.*]

## SPECIFICATIONS

*Of the work to be done and materials to be furnished in the construction of a Stone Dwelling House,* (Design 18,) *at Staten Island, N. Y., for Chas. E. Robins, Esq., in accordance with Plans, Elevations and Details, furnished by D. T. ATWOOD, Architect, 335 Broadway, N. Y.*

### CONDITIONS.

No. 1. The Specifications and the Drawings are intended to co-operate, so that any works exhibited in the Drawings, and not mentioned in the Specifications, or *vice versa*, are to be executed the same as if it were mentioned in the Specifications, and set forth in the Drawings, to the true meaning and intention of the said Drawings and Specifications, without any extra charge whatsoever.

No. 2. All the plans and specifications, working drawings, &c., must be kept in some proper place during the erection of the building. And upon the completion of the same, and before the final certificate is issued, they must be returned to the Architect.

No. 3. All the materials required in the erection of the building, must be of the best of their several kinds, and the work done in a workmanlike manner, according to the several plans and working drawings, and to this specification, and subject to the approval of the Architect, D. T. ATWOOD. No deviation is to be made from the plans and specifications without his full knowledge and consent.

No. 4. The contractors to be responsible for each and every violation of town, village, or city Ordinances, caused by obstructing the streets and sidewalks, and shall hold the owners harmless from any damage or expense arising therefrom ; and at the completion of the work, they shall remove all surplus earth, rubbish and other materials from the streets and premises.

No. 5.   Should any dispute arise respecting the true construction or meaning of the drawings or specifications, the same shall be decided by the Architect, and his decision shall be final and conclusive ; but should any dispute arise respecting the true value of the extra work, or of the works omitted, the same shall be valued by two competent persons—one employed by the owner, and the other by the contractor—and those two shall have power to name an umpire, whose decision shall be binding on all parties.

No. 6.   The carpenter shall furnish to the mason the hights of the respective stories of the building, marked upon a rod for that purpose, setting forth the required hights of the walls.

No. 7.   The *carpenter* and *mason* shall each pay one-third of the cost of insurance on the building during its erection, provided the owner sees fit to effect such insurance, with carpenters' risk, until completion of the building, said owner paying one-third of the premium.

No. 8.   The carpenter shall not be allowed, without the written consent of the owner or architect, to prepare his work in the building.

No. 9.   The expense of cleaning the building, after completion, shall be paid by the carpenter and mason.

No. 10.   The contractors shall afford the architects all required facilities, such as the putting up of ladders and scaffolds, to enable them to inspect the work.

### DIMENSIONS.

The dimensions of main building are as follows :
Width across the front 44 feet.
Depth, front to rear, 42 feet.   Wing building 16 x 23 feet.

| Height of First | Story | 14 feet | 0 inch. | between beams | | |
|---|---|---|---|---|---|---|
| " " Second | " | 12 " | 0 " | " | " | " |
| " " Basement | " | 8 " | 0 " | " | " | " |
| " " Attic | " | 11 " | 0 " | " | | |

in the middle of the building, and 3 feet 6 inches high at the eaves, or from floor beams to wall plate. The style is a modification of the Gothic; the walls to be built of rubble stone, with brown stone dressings for the openings, and quoins for the rubble work. The stone at or near the premises of the owner will be used, he providing a sufficient quantity for this purpose, distributed conveniently near the building site at his own expense.

For the arrangement of rooms, and the general design, see Plans and Elevations, drawn to a scale of ⅛ of an inch for one foot.

### EXCAVATIONS.

Excavate for the whole building according to the plans in form and size, digging to a depth of 3 feet 6 inches from the present surface of the grade, for basement and other walls. Excavate for foctings 20 inches below this depth, or cellar bottom, allowing for a projection of 6 inches on each side of the basement walls. Excavate for a cistern 12 feet in diameter, and 12 feet deep, allowing for an arch 20 inches below the surface. Excavate for a cess-pool, 50 yards from the dwelling, also for a drain communicating with the same from the soil pipes of the building, said cess-pool to be 10 feet deep, and 10 feet in diameter, and the drain to be of a sufficient capacity to receive an 8 inch tile pipe, 30 inches below the surface. Excavate for coal-shoots, and for stoop ʼfoundations and basement area, as directed. Excavate also for a conservatory foundation 3 feet 6 inches below the grade line. When the building is inclosed, use the earth to grade up around it to the bottom of the basement window sills, or to a point 4 feet below the top of the water-table, as shown in the elevation.

### FOOTINGS.

Lay footings under all outside basement walls, 20 inches deep by 34 inches wide, to project 6 inches on either side of said walls, and composed of flat stones as large as can be procured or selected from the other mass of stone. Said footings must be laid in cement mortar composed of hydraulic lime, and clean sharp sand in the usual proportions. Prepare and lay footings under the basement partition walls, 18 inches wide and 18 inches deep, in the same manner.

BASEMENT WALLS.

Lay the outside walls of the basement (starting above the footings) 22 inches thick of rubble stone taken from the site or neighborhood, and in good cement mortar (as above) up to the grade line, and from thence to the top of 1st floor beams in good lime mortar. Make the height of the basement walls from the footings to the top of the water-table 9 feet. Prepare to set back on the basement walls, by a water-table of rough dressed brown stone, from the face thereof for the face of the superstructure, 4 inches. Leave openings in these walls, as per plans and figured working drawings to be hereafter furnished by the Architect. Build Coal-shoots, Stoop Foundations, and area, of rubble stone, laid in cement mortar, the walls to be 18 inches thick, and the shoot and area walls to be coped with 4 inch flagg stone, level with the grade. Provide and fix at each end of the area 6 steps, of flagg stone, 3 inches thick, 10 inches wide, and 4 feet 6 inches long, laid in good stone bearings or strings composed of rubble stone laid in cement. The risers will be composed of brick laid the 4 inch way on stone underpinnings.

Build conservatory foundation walls, as per plan, 18 inches thick, starting 3½ feet below ground, and as high as the basement wall, of rubble stone laid in lime mortar.

Point up all these walls properly both outside and inside, and in laying the wall select stones for face work of a uniform size and color.

Build all the partition walls in the basement of brick, hard burned, laid in good brick mortar, the thickness of walls to be 8 inches; start chimneys in the basement, as directed, to provide for the Dixon Grate, which requires a receptacle for the dust and ashes; make the divisions for apartments in the basement, as per plan. Leave openings and hot air flues, as per plan. Build a vault foundation, as per plan, of rubble stone, walls 18 inches thick, laid in cement, all as directed by the Architect.

### SILLS AND LINTELS.

Provide and fix sills and lintels to all the basement windows, and outside entrance door. The said sills to be of blue stone, 4 inches thick, to project 2 inches from wall face, and all to be the length required by the openings. Sills for the windows to be 8 inches broad, and for the door 24 inches broad, set with a pitch of $\frac{3}{4}$ of an inch. The lintels for windows and door of the basement will be wrought of brown stone, to correspond with the water-table, but those sections of water-table forming lintels will be 12 inches wide on the face, while the water-table proper, will be only 8 inches on the face.

### WATER-TABLE.

Complete the basement walls by topping out with a water-table of brown stone, roughly but acurately dressed, and set flush with the basement wall, and beveled back 4 inches from its face, at which point the superstructure wall will start. Size of water-table 6 x 8 inches. Set all the water-table in cement mortar, and level it up true and straight throughout the whole line. The water-table around the bays will be 12 inches thick by 8 inches high, as the base of the bays is designed to project 10 inches from the wood work. Carry the 8 x 6 inches water-table around the basement of entrance porch, on the stone foundation, 8 inches lower down than on the basement wall of the building [see Elevation]. Point the joints of brown stone with the colored cement usually used. Clean and protect properly this and any other dressed stone work, as directed by the Architect.

### SUPERSTRUCTURE WALLS.

Build the superstructure walls of rubble stone ; the face stones to be selected of uniform size and color, the corners to be trimmed with brown stone quoins, and the openings with brown stone dressings roughly dressed, but accurately formed, for their respective places. The thickness of the walls are to be 18 inches, and are to be laid up in good strong lime mortar, leaving all openings, as per elevations and plans and figured working drawings, to be prepared by the Architect. Turn sustaining arches of brick over all the openings, segmental in form, and strong enough to relieve the lintels and arch stones from any excess of weight. Lay such wooden bonds and lintels as may be required, cut by the carpenter.

Build chimney-breasts where marked on the plan, including a range-breast for the kitchen, enclosing a smoke and ventilating flue for each room, well parged inside. Build all of brick, a good hard merchantable quality. Make the range-breasts 6 feet wide, with 12 inch jambs, and a blue stone or iron lintel. Make all other breasts 5 feet wide, with 16 inch jambs, inclosing 8 x 8 inch flues ; carry out to the roof and top out above the same, as per elevations.

*Fig. 5.*

Half elevation of Chimney top, ⅙ scale.

Make the caps of the two large stacks of brown stone, the balance of face, or rubbed brick. Turn hearth arches between trimmer and header beams against proper skew backs. Lay a range hearth of blue or brown stone 20 x 72 inches over a substantial foundation and arch outside the jambs, lay a brick hearth inside the jambs under the range.

Provide and fix anchors of ¾ inch round wrought iron, 44 inches long, with proper nuts and screws and bed plates, every 10 feet apart in the superstructure walls to secure the plates to the same.

Provide and fix proper anchors for tieing the floor beams to the walls, and any anchors required for dressed stone.

Provide and set dressed brown stone for the superstructure walls as follows: Three door sills to agree with the water-table, each about 24 inches wide, cut, as per detail, the length required by the openings. Sills for 3 bay windows, 6 x 8 inches, plain bevel, 4 inches projection; and 24 gothic sills, 6 x 8 inches, set flush with the wall, of the length required by the respective openings, cut as per detail. Provide 27 segment arches, 6 x 12 inches, with 3 inch beveled jambs, and double this number of caps, 4 inches thick, plain and square, 13 inches long. Trim all the jambs of the openings under these arches with beveled quoins, 10 x 6 inches, as represented by the elevations. Trim the corners of the whole superstructure with quoins, as shown in elevation, either in solid blocks 18 x 24 inches, or with ashlar not less than 4 inches thick.

For particular directions the workmen are referred to the details to be hereafter prepared during the progress of the work. All the dressed brown stone above mentioned, with pediment quoins, and pediment copings, must be laid or set in cement mortar, and properly anchored; and it is intended that none of the brown stone shall be *rubbed*, but roughly tooled or dressed. Carry up the bay windows with stone to the underside of the sills. Point up the stone work in the best manner, using colored mortar for the joints.

### PUGGING.

Provide and lay pugging mortar over "sound boarding," put in by the carpenter, for the first and second floors throughout, composed of coarse mortar mixed with coarse chopped straw or hay; let the pugging be at least $1\frac{1}{2}$ to 2 inches thick, and evenly spread.

### VAULT.

Construct a library vault, as per plan, of 16 inch brick hollow walls, starting on the basement foundation; cover tho top so as to clear the floor beams of second story, with a segmental arch of brick 8 inches thick.  Leave an opening on the library side for an entrance 3 feet wide and 8 feet high, turn an 8 inch arch over the foundation forming the floor, this arch to be covered with cement; the sides of the interior will also be covered or plastered with cement and then kalsomined white; a ventilating flue will be formed to communicate with the chimney flue, with screen, to conduct foul air out of the vault.

### DRAINS.

Construct a principal soil drain from tho water-closet in the basement to the cess-pool in the yard, a distance of 150 feet, of 6 inch tile pipe, laid in the best manner.

Construct 4 inch tile drains for inlet and outlet to the cistern, the outlet to communicate with a separate cess-pool, and be provided with a trap ; place these drains sufficiently below ground to be secure from frost, and let them have a descent of ½ inch to the foot.  Construct around the interior of outside basement walls a drain of 4 inch tile pipe, set over the footing course, and having a gradual descent at a point farthest away from the soil drain towards and connected with the same.  Provide to drain the area by means of this drain, and also the entire cellar, grading the bottom from the middle towards the outside walls.

### FLAGING.

Flag the area with 2 inch flag-stone, laid in good mortar, giving the stones a descent toward the cellar drain so as to discharge any accumulated water at one point.

### BRICK PIERS.

Build brick piers 12 x 12 inches to sustain the porch floor of north front, 5 in number, about 4 feet high.

### LATH, PLASTER,

and hard finish the entire building excepting the attic, cellar, wine, and milk-rooms of the basement story.  The attic story will be finished in two-coat work, not including the *tank* and the *lumber rooms*, which are to be left entirely unfinished. The furring off will be done by the carpenter.

### STUCCO WORK.

Run plain gothic cornices, as per details, around the ceilings of all the principal rooms of 1st and 2d stories, and the main and private halls. The cornice of the 1st floor must be 10 x 12 inches, and those of the 2d floor must be 8 x 10 inches, same style, using as little "stuff" as possible. See details.

Provide and fix for the 1st floor 4 circular gothic centers, 36 inches in diameter, and 2 circular gothic centers 24 inches. For the 2d floor, provide and fix 5 circular gothic centers, 24 inches in diameter.

### VENTILATORS.

Provide and set 9 iron japanned Ventilators, 8 x 8 inches, provided with cords and tassels complete. Provide and fix, as directed, 12 black japanned furnace Registers, of the size directed by the Architect.

### MANTELS AND GRATES.

Provide Mantels or chimney pieces, with Dixon's low down grates complete, for the following rooms: Parlor, one white marble mantel, with the grates set and finished, to cost the sum of 180 dollars. One mantel for Library of verde antique, 160 dollars. One mantel for Living room, black and gold, 150 dollars. One mantel (no grate) for Kitchen, black, 75 dollars. Four for the chambers, green, brown, and sienna, to cost each, including grates and setting, the sum of 160 dollars. If the "Dixon" grates cannot be secured with the mantels inside the above amounts, then any proper substitute or change may be referred to the owner through the Architect.

### CISTERN.

Construct a Cistern, as per plan, 12 feet in diameter, and 12 feet deep in the clear, using rubble stone for the side walls, and hard burned brick for the arch. Lay the arch 24 inches below the surface of the ground; leave a "manhole" in the center, 24 inches square, provided with a stone neck and cover. Plaster the interior of the cistern with 3 coats of water-lime cement, and grout the bottom thoroughly, in the usual manner.

The contractor for the Mason Work will be required to provide sound merchantable materials; to perform all his work in a workmanlike and substantial manner, according to intent and meaning of drawings, and under the Architect's supervision or superintendence. He will be required to protect properly all his finished or unfinished work, and to clear the premises of all rubbish, scaffolding, etc., of his own creating.

———o○ͼ○ͼoo———

## CARPENTER WORK.

### TIMBER AND FRAMING.

Provide spruce and hemlock framing and other timber, of merchantable quality, as follows : Plates 3 x 12 inches, floor beams 3 x 10 inches — 16 inches from centers. Girders 4 x 6 inches and 4 x 8 inches. Partition studs 3 x 4 and 2 x 4 inches ; set the 4 inch way, and 16 inches from centers. Rafters 3 x 6 inches—20 inches from centers. Furrings 2 x 1 — 16 inches from centers. Lintels and bonds 2 x 4 and 2 x 1 inches. Bridging pieces 2 x 4 inches. Bridge all the floors and partitions through the centers. Set all partitions upon horizontal pieces spiked to the floor beams ; and trim 4 x 8 inch girders over the heads of hall and cross partitions, to sustain the floor beams, and carry up partitions with the outside walls. Frame in headers around all the breasts and flues, and opposite all window and door openings in the basement, as directed, and per framing plans, also for stair ways and dumb waiters. Build the attic frame of 4 x 6, 2 x 4 and 6 x 6 inch scantlings, bearing principally upon the middle partitions, well braced, and sufficient to sustain the middle of the roof. Place double studs around all openings. Brace partitions over voids, and double headers over openings, frame for porch, piazza, and bays, as directed.

### ENCLOSING.—SLATING.

Lay the roofs of the building with sound hemlock or spruce boards, edge to edge, and securely nailed to every rafter.

Prepare these roofs to receive the slate, and provide and lay blue and purple slates in 3 alternate courses of blue and purple, underlaid with tarred paper. Provide the small sizes, and lay with galvanized iron nails.

### TIN.

Cover the bays with first quality roofing tin, leaded I. C. laid over narrow mill-worked spruce boards, cover the rear piazza in the same manner.

Provide and fix all manner of flashings for chimneys, bays, porch and piazza, dormer and valley; tin for all valleys painted before being laid down, and securely fixed. Cover all hips and ridges with galvanized iron, securely camped to their respective positions.

### GUTTERS AND LEADERS.

Form tin gutters in the roof around the attic frame, behind the roof balustrade; these gutters are to supply the tank, in the tank room, and must discharge by means of a $3\frac{1}{2}$ inch leader on the east side into the same.

Form gutters of tin for the main roof cornices as large as can be formed by 14 x 20 inch tin, laid the 20 inch way. Provide to discharge the water at the north-east corner of the building into the cistern by a 4 inch tin leader, securely anchored to the wall with iron hooks, and made to connect at the ground with the tile inlet drain to

10*

the cistern. Form small gutters to all bay, porch and piazza roofs, and provide each with one 2 inch leader, discharging at the ground from an elbow into the waste.

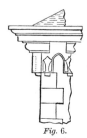

*Fig.* 6.

Eave section of Cornice.
Scale, ⅙ of an inch.

### CORNICES.

Trim the eaves of the main roof with a gothic cornice, as per elevations, whose projection from the walls will be 30 inches, and height on the walls 40 inches.

### OBSERVATORY.

Construct an observatory of wood, with a clear story of 8 feet between beams, as shown in elevations, lighted on all sides by windows, per elevations, 20 x 60 inches each, in 2 lights. Let the projection of the cornice be 20 inches, and the height 18 inches. Trim with a base 18 inches high and 10 inches projection; separate the windows with chamfered pilasters, 9 inches wide; place the roof at an angle of 30 degrees, and surmount its apex with a turned finial, 4 feet high, and 20 inches in diameter at its base. (See details.)

### BAY.

Construct one octagonal bay window, and two square bay windows (per plan), of wood, above the sill course. The pilasters of the parlor bay will be 8 x 8 inches, and chamfered. Those of the square bays will be 12 inches, with 3 inch turned shafts or columns, planted on chamferes formed on the opposite outside angles. Form Boxings under the bay, as directed by the Architect, of mill-worked seasoned stuff, descending from sills to the basement floors, 4 inches in the clear by the width of bays, set plumb, and provided with proper ways, and separate boxes for weights and pulleys. These boxes are to receive the shutters for the bay window inside, in place of the old method.

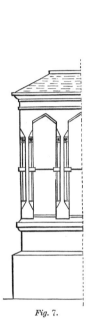

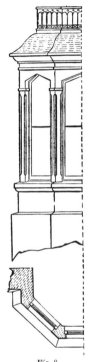

Fig. 7.
Elevation of Square Bay.
Scale, ⅛ of an inch.

Fig. 8.
Elevation of Octagonal Bay.
Scale, ⅛ of an inch.

PORCH.

Build a front porch of wood, as shown, with a narrow pine, mill-worked, floor, joints laid in white lead, with pedestal base, surmounted by square pilaster backs and ¾ round, 10 inch pilasters planted against said backs, and all supporting an entablature and roof over tudor arches, as shown. The thickness of the base or pedestal is 15 inches, and of the ground and pilaster 12 inches; the interior is plainly finished and sheathed with narrow beaded ceiling boards not over 3 inches wide; the exterior is to be covered with narrow 3 x 1¼ inch mill-worked boards, and above the caps of columns made to represent stone courses, by means of chamfer grooves. Project the cornice from the body or face of the porch 24 inches, and let its height be 22 inches. Provide and fix a balustrade (as shown) 28 inches high, with clustered pedestals 8 x 8 inches each, and 8 x 8 inch quarter foil balusters, set 20 inches apart, and filled in with ornamental wrought iron wire panels. Surmount the caps of corner pedestals with gothic points.

The roof of porch will be covered with tin; and preparations for gutters must be previously made by the carpenter, as directed; pitch the roof 4 inches from the center. (Size of porch 6 x 12 feet.)

*Fig.* 9.

Elevation of entrance Porch.
Scale, ¼ of an inch.

### STOOP, &c.

Attached to the porch will be the stoop and steps. The former will be 4 x 12 feet, made of wood, sheathed up over a rough frame on the outside with narrow mill-worked pine 1¼ inch plank, and floored with the same. The lattice 4 x 8 inch, or, including 4 steps and 5 risers, 12 inches broad, and 8 inches high, and 8 feet long, constructed in the usual manner with 1½ inch pine treads and 1 inch risers, and fixed to plank strings inside of dressed 1¼ inch risers, and sheathed up and down on the outside under the strings with 1 inch narrow boards, mill-worked, and laid on a rough frame; surmount the stoop with newels and rails, as shown ; the intermediate spaces to be filled in with ornamental wrought iron wire panels. Size of the step newells 10 x 10 inches, and 3 feet 6 inches high; size of stoop newels, 8 x 8 inches, and 2 feet 10 inches high ; width of rails, 12 inches; thickness, 6 inches; size of base, 4 x 6 inches.

### OUTSIDE STEPS.

Build outside steps for the conservatory, kitchen entrance and rear piazza, in the same manner as specified for stoop steps ; for widths, number of risers, &c., see plans and elevations.

### PIAZZA.

Build a rear piazza over the basement area, as per plans and eievations, 8 x 26 feet, and 15 feet high. Lay the floor of 1¼ inch mill-worked pine [in white lead] over a rough timber frame of 3 x 10 inch beams, 16 inches from centers, resting on the brick piers, and ceiled underneath and on the outside, as directed. Support the roof with 10 x 10 inch chamfered pillars, trimmed with a base, necking, and caps. Form the frieze of 2 inch pine plank; let the roof project 24 inches, and rise 22 inches. Plane and bead the rafters (which are to be 2 x 6 inches, placed 18 inches from centers), and cover the same with narrow beaded ceiling boards, with the dressed sides downwards, upon which the tin will be laid. Construct the pillars out of 1½ inch seasoned pine plank.

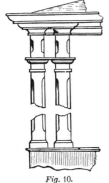

*Fig.* 10.
Sections of Rear Piazza, ⅛ scale.

### ROOF BALUSTRADE.

Provide and fix a roof balustrade, as shown, extending around the observatory and over the pediment, composed of a plain pattern of wrought iron wire railing, fixed between six 18 x 18 inch wooden pedestals, 24 inches high, surmounted with square caps, and pyramidal gothic points 24 inches high, and the whole fixed to a base 4 inches thick, and 18 inches broad, made of wood to correspond with the coping of the stone pediment; behind this the tank gutters will be formed, as before mentioned.

## BALCONIES.

*Fig. 11.*
Section of Roof Balustrade.
Scale, ⅛ of an inch.

Provide and fix wrought iron wire balconies, 2 feet 6 inches high, supported by iron brackets set in the wall, (excepting the one over the parlor bay) and provide with wooden floors of narrow 1½ inch pine plank, secured to the brackets with screws; trim the edges of the floors with a nose and a cove, making the height of the margin 4 inches; two of said balconies will be square, and 30 inches wide by 7 feet 6 inches long; the other one will be octagonal. [See plans.]

## DORMERS.

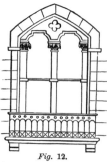

*Fig. 12.*
Elevation of Balcony Window.
Scale, ⅛ of an inch.

Build four triangular Dormers on each side of the roof, lighting the attic, 7 feet wide at the base, and 5 feet 6 inches altitude, or high, outside measurement; slope the roofs at an angle of 60 degrees. Trim the fronts with crown mouldings and verge boards. Slate the roofs and surmount the ridges with wrought iron wire finials, 18 inches high, painted bronze and gilded. Form casements inside, to receive swinging sashes, as directed.

### DOOR AND WINDOW FRAMES.

Provide and set plank window frames for the basement, of the sizes required by the openings, (excepting laundry frames, which are to have boxes for weights), construct of 2 inch plank, for jambs, and 1½ inch plank for

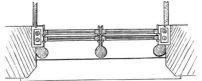

*Fig.* 13.—Section of Window Frames.  Scale, ½ of an inch.

sills, case with a plain Gothic bead, make the mullions, of. such as require the same, 3 and 2 inches thick, as directed. Make all the window jambs 7 inches wide, the outside door jambs, 18 inches wide and paneled, a portion of which may be ceiled.  Inside door jambs 6 inches wide, and 1¼ inches thick.  Provide and set 4 window frames with mullions, as shown, with boxes for weights, and 6 inch turned columns, supporting quarter foil arches, under "tudor" stone arches, (see details).  Provide and set all other window frames, both single and mullioned, of the sizes required by the openings, with boxes for weights made in the usual manner, and cased on the outside with a 2 inch Gothic bead. (See elevations, also details).  Provide and fix all outside door frames of the sizes required by the openings, made of 2 inch pine plank, with paneled jambs, corresponding with the door panels, and moulded with ogee flush moulds. Case outside of door frames with 2 inch Gothic beads. Make interior door frames of 1¼ inch pine, 6 inches wide; the outside door frames to be 18 inches wide.

### SASHES AND DOORS.

Provide double glazed 2 inch sashes for the basement, those of the laundry to be hung with weights, and all the remainder to be hung with hinges and fastened with bolts. (No. of lights, 1 and 2 in each sash).  Provide single glazed 2 inch sashes for the first, second, and attic stories, of two and four lights, as per elevations, hung with weights and fastened with No. 27 sash fasteners, in a complete manner. The attic sashes will swing on hinges, and be fastened with bolts or buttons. The observatory sash will be hung, as others in first and second stories, and made to slide down in boxes under sill of windows. All sashes throughout the building, will be glazed with double thick American glass, first quality.

### DOORS.

Provide doors as follows : *First story*—One pair front doors 5 feet 11 inches, two panels, R. M., 2½ inches thick, and glazed. One pair rear doors, 5 feet 11 inches, two panels, R. M., 2½ inches thick, and glazed. One pair dining-room doors, 6 feet 11 inches, eight panels, R. M., 2 inches thick. Eleven single doors, 3 by 10 feet, 4 panels, R. M , 2 inches thick. *Second story*—Eighteen single doors, 2 feet 10 inches by 9 feet, four paneled, ogee joints, 1½ inches thick. *Attic and Basement*—Nineteen single doors, 2 feet 10 inches by 7 feet 6 inches, four paneled, ogee joints, 1½ inches thick. One pair basement doors 5 x 7 feet, four paneled, ogee joints, 1½ inches thick, and glazed. Provide and fix dumb-waiter, water-closet, and hall-closet doors, as directed, four paneled, ogee joints, 1½ inches thick. All to be of clear, seasoned, white pine, made in the best manner, and the work to be kiln-dried before gluing up. Hang all the basement and attic doors with 3½ x 3½ inch loose joint butt hinges; trim and fasten with 5 inch mortise locks and white mineral furniture. Hang the first floor doors with 5 x 5 inch loose joint butt hinges ; trim and fasten with 5½ inch mortise locks with porcelain furniture. The entrance doors to have 7 inch mortise locks, with night keys, and also flush iron bolts. The second story doors to be hung with 4 x 4 inch loose joint butt hinges, and fastened and trimmed like the first story.

### FLOORS.

Lay all the floors of the basement, first and second stories, with narrow 1¼ x 4 inch mill-worked pine plank. No wooden floors are to be laid in the cellars, wine, or milk rooms; but in the other portions locust sleepers will be laid down, 20 inches apart, to receive the floor planks. Lay the attic floors of wide, mill-worked spruce, 1¼ inches thick. Lay the conservatory floor of the same, over 3 x 8 inch beams, 18 inches from centers.

### PARTITIONS.

Form all the partitions above the basement of 2 x 4 inch studs, set the 4 inch way, 16 inches from centers, over horizontal pieces of the same laid on the floors. Form principal rooms and closets, as per plans; double the studs around all openings, and bridge all the partitions through the middle with 2 x 4 inch studs.

### FURRING.

Furr off all the outside walls with 2 x 1 inch spruce furring strips, 16 inches from centers, secured to the top and bottom, and at two points equi-distant in the middle. Furr down or strap the first and second story ceilings with the same materials, the same distance apart, nailing to every joist or beam.

### STAIRS.

Build one flight of main front stairs, 3½ feet wide, with 7 inch risers, and 10 inch treads, in the usual manner, of pine, 1¼ inch treads, quarter circle at the landing, with a 12 inch well-hole, surmounted with a 6 inch toad-back rail, 2 inch octagonal balusters, square top and bottom, and a 12 inch octagonal newel, with turned cap and base. Build three flights of stairs, (private back,) starting from the basement, and landing in the attic, quarter circle, and 2 feet 9 inches wide, with a 6 inch well-hole, and surmounted with a plain and oval 3 inch black walnut rail, 1¼ inch turned spindle balusters, and turned 8 inch newel, at the starting.

The rail will be continued around the cylinder and " die," against the wall in the attic passage. Stud off and form niches, as per plans. When the rails are properly completed and hung, the stairs bracketed, etc., polish or rub the rails, newels, and balusters, and oil two coats, in the best manner. Build a flight of attic stairs, 2 feet 6 inches wide, surmounted with a pine rail, as directed, to observatory.

BASE AND ARCHITRAVES.

Provide and fix plain 5 inch single moulded architraves for the basement story. Wainscot the laundry and passages. Provide and fix throughout the first and second stories 4 and 5 inch gothic cove and bead architraves, fixed

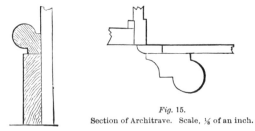

*Fig.* 15.
Section of Architrave. Scale, ⅛ of an inch.

*Fig.* 14.
Section of Base. Scale, ⅛ of an inch.

to grounds behind plain jambs. Place panel backs and plain elbows under the sills of all the windows. Lay base throughout first and second stories of the building (excepting kitchen) 8 inches wide, with a plain plinth 1 inch thick, and capped with a Gothic roll or bead to correspond with that of the architrave. Trim the attic in the same manner as specified.

WAINSCOT.

Skirt the kitchen with a plain wainscot, 3 feet high, all

around, composed of narrow beaded ceiling boards, capped with a nose and cove. Wainscot the laundry and the basement passages in the same manner.

### SHUTTERS.

Provide and hang in the usual manner 1¼ inch ogee joint shutters, paneled both sides, for first and second stories, hung in 6 inch folds for each window, trimmed and fastened in the usual manner with knobs and bolts, or hasps. The bay window shutters will be hung in boxes with weights, one fold to each light, 1¼ inches thick, and ironed on the edges to secure from warping. See Architect's details and special directions.

### DUMB WAITER.

Provide and fix a way for a dumb waiter, from the basement to the second story, 24 x 16 inches in the clear, perfectly true and smooth, ceiled with narrow matched boards, 3 inches wide. Provide and hang in this way, a waiter closet in the usual manner, with all the necessary apparatus complete.

### FITTINGS AND FIXTURES.

Fit up with pine wood around the water closets, bath tub, and wash bowl; around the former with plain paneling, and around the latter with plain narrow-beaded ceiling. Case around all plumber's piping, as directed. Fit up a linen closet, as per plan, with shelves, drawers, and a cedar inclosure, 20 x 40 inches, for furs and silks. Fit up all other clothes closets with two shelves and two dozen japanned wardrobe hooks each. Fit up the kitchen pantry with 8 shelves, 12 and 18 inches wide, and a case of four drawers, 6 inches deep, trimmed with locks and knobs. Fit up the closet marked *c*, with broad shelves, 5 in number, with a napkin drawer under the first one, trimmed with a strong lock and knobs.

Fix on strong cleets one dozen wardrobe hooks for each servant's bedroom, for the dressing room, and for the bath room, and 1½ dozen for the closet under the main back stairs.

### TANK ROOM.

Strengthen the floors of the tank room, by doubling the number of the beams, 2 to 1 for those specified in "Timber and Framing," and then construct a tank 8 x 12 feet, and 4 feet high, of narrow mill-worked plank drove together in a frame-work of 4 x 4 inch joists, and clamped all around its outer surface every 24 inches (see details). No cover is needed; but precaution must be taken to secure it from freezing by making the room air tight.

### BELLS AND SPEAKING TUBES.

Provide and hang 10 bells in the kitchen to communicate with the first and second floors, as follows:—One for front entrance, one for parlor, one for library, one for living room, and one for each of the principal chambers or bed rooms on the second floor, and fix one designated a " foot-bell," in the center of dining room floor, all properly adjusted, and radiating from the kitchen. Also provide and fix speaking tubes from the second story, adjoining the dumb waiter, communicating with the laundry and kitchen. Provide and hang a bell in the servants' room communicating with the bed room over the living room on second floor.

### VAULT RAIL, &C.

Provide and fix a library wrought iron railing, 3½ feet high, with an entrance gate, 3 feet wide, opposite the vault door, as designated on plan. Provide and fix an iron frame, and iron doors, to the vault, as directed. These doors and frame the owner will provide at his own expense. Hang a wooden R. M. 4 paneled pine door, over these iron doors, as directed.

### DUST-HOLE.

Provide and fix in the kitchen, to communicate with the coal and wood cellar a dust leader, 6 inches in diameter, made of tin or sheet iron, and painted, provided with a funnel-shaped mouth 12 inches in diameter, and covered with a lid, as directed.

### PLUMBING.

Provide for the plumbing supply as follows:—Two large size iron sinks, set on legs, one in the kitchen, and one in the laundry. Build four wash-trays in the laundry, 20 x 24 inches—18 inches deep, and supplied with hot and cold water pipes. Provide and fix a good $2\frac{1}{2}$ inch brass force-pump in the laundry, communicating both with the cistern and the tank, with lead or iron $1\frac{1}{4}$ inch pipes. Provide and fix a complete water closet apparatus, and a urinal in the basement, as per plan. Provide and set on an iron stand a 45 gallon copper boiler, square head, and connect with the water-back of the range (supplied by the owner). Provide both sinks with hot and cold water. Provide for the bath room one copper-pinced bath tub, 5 feet 6 inches long ; one wash-bowl set in a marble frame, with marble wall plates, as per plan, and both the tub and bowl supplied with hot and cold water. Provide for the bath room, one water closet, with all its apparatus, in complete working order. Provide and fix a 4 inch iron soil-pipe in the wall, descending from the bath room to sewer drain. Line the tank, in the tank room, with copper in the best manner, supply all necessary traps, waste and supply pipes, overflow pipes, and all other materials, necessary to make a complete and satisfactory job. Provide plaited cocks for the wash-bowl.

### PAINTING.

Paint all exterior wood work, except window frames, three coats, of warm stone gray color, thoroughly sanded, using lead and oil for the last two coats. Paint or stain the outside of the window frames two coats of cherry or oak color. Paint all sashes outside a bronze green. Paint the parlor and the bed rooms three coats of pure white. Paint the attic and the basement two coats of French gray Grain the dining room, halls, library, living-room, kitchen, and pantry in imitation of oak wood. Paint all the closets two coats of white lead and oil paint. Before painting any of the work, nail-heads must be covered with putty, crevices must be filled, knots shellaced, and the work thoroughly rubbed and sand-papered. Paint all the tin roofs, valleys, gutters, and leaders two coats of slate colored paint, as directed.

### MATERIALS.

Materials of every kind must be of a good merchantable quality. The wood for finishing the building to be principally of white pine, thoroughly seasoned, and all the work to be completed in a thoroughly workmanlike manner, to the full intent and meaning of drawings, scale, and detail, and under the directions of the Architect.

The carpenter will be required to properly protect his work during its progress, and at its completion, to remove all rubbish of his own creating from the premises, as directed.

### MISCELLANEOUS.

Provide and fix iron gratings to the basement windows above the grade line, as directed. Provide gratings for the glazed doors. Shutters must be provided for the laundry windows, of wood, $1\frac{1}{4}$ inches thick.

### CONSERVATORY.

Build a conservatory of wood and glass, 13 x 16 feet, as per plan and elevation; the roof curved and pitched at an angle of $22°$; the sash bars curved, $1$ x $2\frac{1}{2}$ inches, set 12 inches apart between rebates; and the whole house glazed with single thick American glass laid in aquaria cement. Provide one outside entrance, three roof and three side ventilating sashes, provided with proper hold-fast fixtures, complete. Trim the eaves with neat moulds, projecting 6 inches, and form a light gutter therein, discharging the water to the ground by means of a 2 inch leader. Paint the whole house two coats of white lead and oil paint, inside and outside. Inside stands and tables are to be provided by the owner. For the construction, see details.

### HOT AIR.

Chambers or pipes must be inserted in the partitions for first and second stories, as per plans, of the proper capacity to supply twelve outlets, or registers. Provide and set in the basement hall one of Lisley & Elliot's No. 10 Gothic furnaces, for hot air supply, set in a brick chamber in the usual manner, with hot air pipes radiating to, and communicating with the register pipes. Provide a cold air box, as directed, made of mill-worked stuff, 1 inch thick, 12 x 24 inches.

### GAS PIPES.

Provide and lay pipes of the proper capacity, to supply the basement with four outlets, the first floor with eight outlets, and the second floor with eight outlets, as directed.

*Fig.* 16.
Half Elevation of Observatory.
Scale ⅛ of an inch.

## Design Nineteen.

# A DOUBLE COTTAGE, IN THE RURAL GOTHIC STYLE.

———o◦;◦;o◦———

THE demand of late for double dwellings has been so frequent, that we feel we shall be doing somebody a service by the introduction of the following design:

To those who possess only moderate means, with the desire to make the most of them, this class of dwelling has advantages of considerable merit over the single dwelling.

The most important is that of cost; since by joining two small houses together, not only is an entire flank wall saved, but the expense of another is greatly reduced, while the effect of a large dwelling is secured, by the usual accompaniment of external area, and architectural

*Fig.* 1.

11

detail, and reducing probably the entire cost twenty-five per cent. below the cost of two se arate dwellings.

Fig. 1.—Elevation of entrance front, 42½ feet wide, and two stories and an attic in height. Height of first story, 10 feet; second story, 9 feet; whole depth from front to rear, 59 feet; extension, one story high. The walls of this dwelling are filled in with pale brick, lathed and plastered inside, and weather-boarded outside. The gables are trimmed with ornamental verge boards, cut out of 2 inch plank. The finials are octagonal, 7 inches in diameter. Ornamental balconies, 30 inches wide, project over the entrances; side stoops and hoods are provided for the side doors. Piazzas were purposely left off to lessen the cost, but can be added on each end of the main building. The entire finish is of medium quality, and thoroughly substantial. Hard wood mantels are provided for the first story, flue rings and shelves for the second story. The chimnies are toped out above the roof with Garnkirk octagonal shafts. Cost of the entire building, $4000, or $2000 a dwelling.

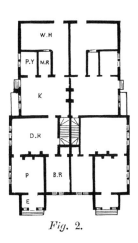

*Fig.* 2.

Fig. 2.—First floor. Size of the main building, $25\frac{1}{2}$ x $42\frac{1}{2}$ feet; rear building, $33\frac{1}{2}$ x $33\frac{1}{2}$ feet. F, lobby, paved with tile, 6 x 7 feet; P, parlor, 12 x 12 feet; B, R, bed-room, 8 x 12 feet; D, R, dining-room, 12 x 16 feet; K, kitchen, 14 x 16 feet; P, Y, pantry, 6 x 8 feet; M, R, milk or store-room, 4 x 8 feet; W, H, wood-house, 12 x 16 feet. The stairs are "box," with cellar flights underneath.

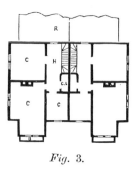

*Fig.* 3.

Fig, 3.—Second floor. C, C, C, chambers, 12 x 12, 12 x 18, and 8 x 10 feet. The front chamber opens in the front upon the balcony.

## Design Twenty.

## ITALIAN COTTAGE.

———◦❀◦———

Fig. 1.—Front elevation, $\frac{1}{16}$ of an inch for one foot.

Fig. 2.—First floor plan.

### REFERENCE.

P, parlor, 14 x 20 feet ; S, R, sitting and reception room, 10 x 14 feet ; C, bed-chamber, 10 x 10 feet; B, R, bath room, 6 x 10 feet; D, R, dining room, 12 x 15 feet ; P, pantry, 6 x 6 feet; I, C, ice closet, 6 x 6 feet ; K, kitchen, 9 x 13 feet ; W, H, and W, R, wood house and wash room, 8 x 15 feet; L, lobby, 7 x 9 feet; A, arcade, 7 x 19 feet.

*Fig.* 1.

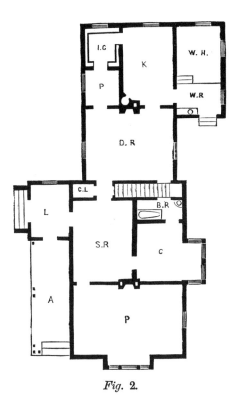

*Fig.* 2.

Fig. 3.—Second floor ; containing three bed rooms, $10 \times 20$, $10 \times 16$, and $9 \times 14$ feet respectively. Closets per plan; and a room in the upper story of the tower $9 \times 9$ feet. Cost of House, $5000.

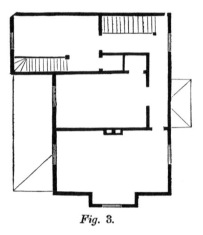

*Fig.* 3.

# Design Twenty-One.

## ITALIAN VILLA.

——◦◦⦂◦⦂◦◦——

Fig. 1.—Front elevation, $\frac{1}{16}$ of an inch for one foot.

Fig. 2.—First floor.

### REFERENCES.

P, parlor, 15 x 18 feet ; D, R, dining room, 12 x 18 feet. The hall separating these rooms is 7 x 18 feet; stairs 3 feet wide. S, R, sitting room, 14 x 14 feet ; L, larder or pantry, 6 x 8 feet, with a side-board (S, B) ; W, C, wash or toilet closets, 5 x 6 feet; W, C, W, C, outside and inside water closets, $3\frac{1}{2}$ x 4 feet wide ; P, Y, pantry, 8 x 8 feet ; M, R, milk room, 4 x 8 feet ; W, H, wood house, 10 x 12 feet ; P, J,

11*

*Fig.* 1.

conservatory, 12x36 feet; opening into sitting room by glass doors.

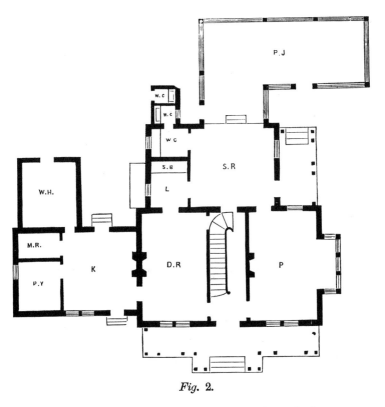

*Fig.* 2.

Fig. 3.—Second floor. C, C, C, C, bed chambers, 12x18, 12x13, 11x14, and 11x11 feet; H, hall, 7x18 feet, with stairs continuous to

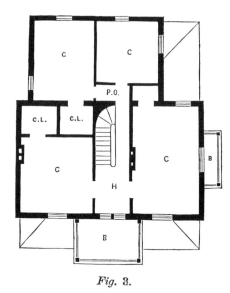

*Fig.* 3.

servants attic; C, L, closets, 5 x 6 feet; B, B, balconies, 7 x 12 and 3 x 9 feet. There is a cellar under the whole building 7 feet high. Cost, $8000.

## Design Twenty-Two.

### MELROSE COTTAGES.

FOR P. MC HUGH, ESQ.

———o○○○○○○——

Fig. 1.—Front elevation, $\frac{1}{32}$ of an inch for one foot.

Fig. 2.—First floor plan.

#### REFERENCES.

P, parlor, 14 x 13½ feet; B, P, back parlor, 14 x 13½ feet; S, study, 6 x 8 feet; H, lobby

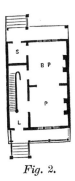

*Fig. 2.*

*Fig.* 1.

or hall, 6 x 21 feet. Piazzas front and rear, 6 feet wide.

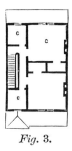

*Fig.* 3.

Fig. 3.—Second floor. C,C,C,C, bed rooms, 13 x 13 and 7 x 8 feet.

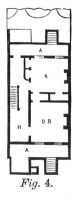

*Fig.* 4.

Fig. 4.—Basement. H, hall, 6 feet wide; D, R, dining room, 13 x 13 feet; K, kitchen, 13 x 13 feet, with three closets; A, A, front and rear areas. Cost, $2,500 each house.

## Design Twenty-Three.

## A PICTURESQUE VILLA.

### DESIGNED FOR MR. TOOKER, OF ORANGE, N. J.

————◦○○○○◦——

Fig. 1.—Front elevation, $\frac{1}{24}$ of an inch for one foot.

Fig. 2.—First floor.

### REFERENCES.

T, tower, 8 x 8 feet; H, hall, separated by an arch, 8 x 8 feet, with a back corridor communicating therewith, 4 feet wide; P, parlor, 15 x 20 feet; D, R, dining room, 12 x 15 feet; L, library, 10 x 11 feet; K, kitchen, 14 x 15 feet, with pantries; P, P, side and rear piazzas, 8 x 10 feet.

Second floor contains 5 rooms and 4 closets. Attic 2 servants' rooms. A cellar is built un-the whole dwelling, 7 feet high.

*Fig.* 1.

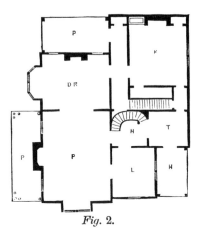

*Fig.* 2.

First story, 11 feet high ; second story, 11 feet high ; attic, 9 feet high, in the middle. Designed for stone, with slate roofs, at a cost of $10,000.

## Design Twenty-Four.

# A DOUBLE SUMMER RESIDENCE, OF BRICK, ON THE BAY SHORE, S. I.

### DESIGNED FOR MR. COVILLE.

Fig. 1.—Elevation of the water front, $\frac{1}{32}$ of an inch for one foot.

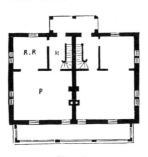

*Fig.* 2.

Fig. 2.—First floor.

### REFERENCES.

H, hall, 8 x 12 feet; R, R, reception room, 12 x 12 feet; P, parlor, 16 x 20 feet.

*Fig.* 1.

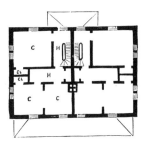

*Fig.* 3.

Fig. 3.—Second floor. H, upper hall, 8 x 12 feet ; C, C, C, bed rooms, 12 x 12 and 10 x 10 feet ; C, L. closets.

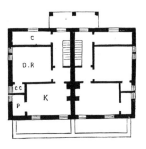

*Fig.* 4.

Fig. 4.—Basement. C, cellar, 3 x 13 feet ; D, R, dining room, 12 x 14 feet ; K, kitchen, 12 x 16 feet ; P, pantry, and C, C, china closet.

Each house or dwelling to cost $4000.

## Design Twenty-Five.

## A COUNTRY HOUSE.

———◦o✠o◦———

FIG. 1.—Perspective view, $\frac{1}{24}$ of an inch for one foot.

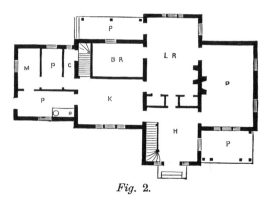

*Fig. 2.*

Fig. 2.—First floor.

### REFERENCES.

H, hall, 13 x 13 feet; P, parlor, 14 x 20 feet; L, R, living room, 13 x 18 feet; K, kitchen,

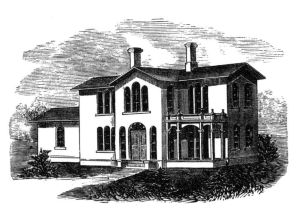

Fig. 1.

12 x 16 feet; B, R, bed room, 8 x 12 feet; P, passage; C, passage to cellar; P, pantry, 5 x 10 feet; M, milk room, 7 x 10 feet; P, P, piazzas, front and rear.

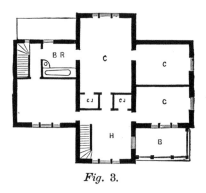

*Fig.* 3.

Fig. 3.—Second floor. H, hall, 13 x 13 feet; C, C, C, C, bed rooms, 10 x 14, 13 x 18, and 11 x 16 feet; B, R, bath room, 8 x 9 feet; C, L, closets; B, balcony.

Designed to be built of brick. Cost, $10,000.

## Design Twenty-Six.

## A SINGLE SUMMER RESIDENCE OF BRICK, BAY SHORE, S. I.

### DESIGNED FOR MR. COVILLE.

———◦○❖○○———

Fɪɢ. 1.—Elevation of water front. Scale, $\frac{1}{16}$ of an inch for one foot.

*Fig.* 2.

Fig. 2.—First floor.

### REFERENCES.

H, hall, $7\frac{1}{2}$ x 10 feet; L, living room, 18 x 18 feet; L, library, 10 x 10 feet.

12

*Fig.* 1.

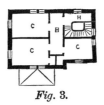

*Fig.* 3.

Fig. 3.—Second floor. H, hall, $7\frac{1}{2}$ x 10 feet; side hall 4 feet wide; C, C, C, bed rooms, 9 x 13 and 10 x 10 feet.

*Fig.* 4.

Fig. 4.—Basement. H, hall, $7\frac{1}{2}$ x 10 feet; D, dining or breakfast room; K, kitchen, 12 x 16 feet; C, cellar, 6 x 9 feet; C, C, closets for stores and wine.

Cost, $5000

## Design Twenty-Seven.

## A MECHANIC'S COTTAGE.

Fig. 1.—Front elevation. Scale, $\frac{1}{16}$ of an inch for one foot.

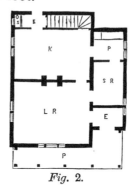

*Fig.* 2.

Fig. 2.—First floor.

E, entry, 4 x 7 feet; L, R, living room, 11 x 13 feet; K, kitchen, 11 x 13 feet; E, back entry; S, sink and pump; S, R, store room, 5 x 7 feet; P, pantry, 5 x 5 feet; P, piazza.

*Fig.* 1.

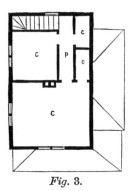

*Fig.* 3.

Fig. 3.—Second floor.  C, C,  bed rooms, 8 x 9  and  11 x 13  feet;  P, C, C,  closets and passage, per plan.

Built of wood, at a cost of $1400.

## 𝔇𝔢𝔰𝔦𝔤𝔫 𝔗𝔴𝔢𝔫𝔱𝔶-𝔈𝔦𝔤𝔥𝔱.

## A COUNTRY HOUSE.

—◦◦✖◦◦—

F𝖨G. 1.—Front elevation.   Scale, $\frac{1}{32}$ of an inch for one foot.

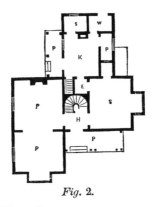

*Fig. 2.*

Fig. 2.—First floor.

REFERENCES.

H, hall, 8 feet wide; P, P, parlors, 14 x 16 and 16 x 16 feet; S, sitting and dining room,

*Fig.* 1.

16 x 18 feet; E, entry or lobby, 5 x 5 feet; K, kitchen, 12 x 15 feet; W, wood-house, 5 x 8 feet; S, store room, 5 x 8 feet; P, kitchen pantry, 4 x 9 feet; P, piazzas.

Second floor has 5 rooms and 4 closets.

Built of wood, and to cost $6000.

## Design Twenty-Nine.

## BRONXVILLE HOUSE.

### DESIGNED FOR FRANCIS BACON, ESQ.

Fig. 1.—Perspective view.   Scale, $\frac{1}{40}$ of an inch for one foot.

*Fig. 2.*

Fig. 2.—First floor.

### REFERENCES.

H, hall, 13 x 17 feet;  P, parlor, 15 x 17 feet;  S, R, sitting room, 15 x 17 feet;  D, R,

*Fig.* 1.

dining room, 13 x 17 feet; K, kitchen, 13½ x 15 feet; W, R, wash room, 6 x 10 feet; P, Y, pantry, 6 x 6 feet; S, store room, 4 x 4½ feet; W, H, wood house, 5 x 15 feet.

*Fig.* 3.

Fig. 3.—Second floor. C, C, C, C, C, bed chambers, 14 x 15, 15 x 15, 11 x 13, 10½ x 13, and 9 x 10 feet; B, R, bath room, 7½ x 9½ feet; S, R, servants' room, 8 x 10 feet; H, hall.

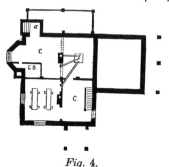

*Fig.* 4.

Fig. 4.—Basement.   A, area;   C, C, cellar ; C, B, coal bin.

Designed to be built of stone, and to cost $12,000.

## 𝔇esign 𝔗hirty.

## A COUNTRY HOUSE.

DESIGNED FOR MR. COLE, SNEEDEN'S LANDING,

ON THE HUDSON.

FIG. 1.—Front elevation.   Scale, $\frac{1}{24}$ of an inch for one foot.

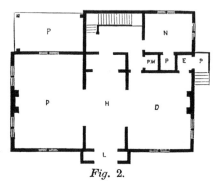

*Fig.* 2.

Fig. 2.—First floor.

REFERENCES.

L, lobby or vestibule; H, hall, 10 x 24 feet; P, parlor, 18 x 24 feet; D, dining room, 17 x 20

*Fig.* 1.

feet; N, nursery, 10 x 12 feet; P, piazza, 9½ x 18 feet; D, W, waiter; P, pantry; E, entry from side porch.

Second story contains five bed rooms and closets.

The above, although designed for wood, we learn, was executed in stone, with full second story, and have no knowledge of the cost. If built, as designed, of wood, with basement below first floor, its cost would not be far from $8000.

## Design Thirty-One.

## MR. J. H. POST'S VILLA.

### DESIGNED FOR ERECTION AT GLASTENBURY, CONN.

FIG. 1.—Front elevation. Scale, $\frac{1}{32}$ of an inch for one foot.

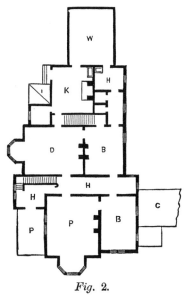

*Fig.* 2.

Fig. 2.—First floor.

*Fig.* 1.

REFERENCES.

P, piazza; H, hall, $11\frac{1}{2}$ x $12\frac{1}{2}$ feet; P, parlor, 18 x 20 feet; B, library or bed room,
12 x 18 feet; C, conservatory; D, dining room,
16 x 20 feet; B, bed room, 14 x 16 feet; K,
kitchen, 14 x 16 feet; W, wood house, 14 x 16
feet; H, bathing room, 8 x 10 feet; closets per
plan.

*Fig.* 3.

Fig. 3.—Second floor. C, C, C, C, C, C, bed
rooms; B, bath room.

Designed for wood, and to cost $15,000.

## Design Thirty-Two.

## A SUBURBAN DWELLING OF STONE.

——◦◦❁◦◦——

Fig. 1.—Perspective view.   Scale, $\frac{1}{24}$ of an inch for one foot.

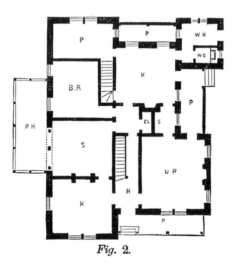

*Fig. 2.*

Fig. 2.—First floor.

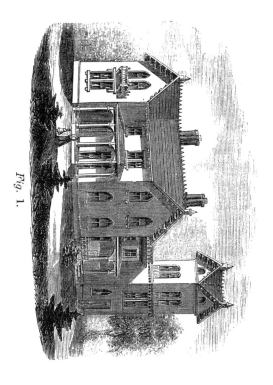

Fig. 1.

REFERENCES.

H, hall; P, parlor, 14 x 15 feet; S, study, 14 x 15 feet; P, H, plant house; D, R, dining room, 16 x 18 feet; K, kitchen, 14 x 16 feet; P, pantry, 9 x 15 feet; B, R, bed room, 11 x 14 feet; C, L, closets; S, side-board; W, H, coals and wood; W, C, water closet; P, P, piazzas.

Second floor contains five rooms and closets. Cost, about $15,000.

*Fig.* 1.

(Design Thirty-three.—See next page.)

## Design Thirty-Three.

## LABORER'S COTTAGE.

————

Fig. 1.—Front elevation.   Scale, $\frac{1}{32}$ of an inch for one foot.

*Fig.* 2.

Fig. 2.—First floor.

P, porch, 10 x 10 feet; E, entry or lobby, 8 x 8 feet; L, living room, 16 x 20 feet; K, kitchen, 16 x 20 feet; B, B, bed rooms, 10 x 12 and 10 x 10 feet; C, C, closets, 8 x 8 and 4 x 5 feet; P, pantry, 5 x 5 feet.

Cost, built of wood, $1500.